Developing Pre-School Communication and Language

D1380200

SWINDON COLLEGE

LEARNING RESOURCE CENTRE

About the authors

Chris Dukes is a qualified teacher with over 20 years' experience. She has worked in various London primary schools as a class teacher and later as a member of the Senior Management Team. Chris has a Masters degree in Special Needs and through her later role as a SENCO and support teacher, many years' experience of working with children with a variety of needs. Chris has worked closely with staff teams, mentoring, advising and supervising work with children with additional needs, as well as with other education and health professionals. Chris currently works as an Area SENCO supporting Special Needs Coordinators and managers in a wide range of pre-school settings. As well as advising, she writes courses, delivers training and produces publications.

Maggie Smith began her career as a nursery teacher in Birmingham. She has worked as a peripatetic teacher for an under 5s EAL Team and went on to become the Foundation Stage manager of an Early Years Unit in Inner London. Maggie helped to set up an innovative unit for young children with behavioural difficulties and has also worked supporting families of children with special needs. Maggie has taught on Early Years BTEC and CACHE courses at a college of higher education. She currently works as an Area SENCO supporting Special Needs Coordinators and managers in a wide range of pre-school settings. As well as advising she, writes courses, delivers training and produces publications.

Developing Pre-School Communication and Language

SWINDON COLLEGE

LEARNING RESOURCE CENTRE

Chris Dukes and Maggie Smith

Illustrations by Simon Smith

P·C·P

Paul Chapman
Publishing

© Chris Dukes and Maggie Smith 2007
Illustrations © Sage 2007

First published 2007

Apart from any fair dealing for the purposes of research or private study, or criticism or review, as
permitted under the Copyright, Designs and Patents Act, 1988, this publication may be reproduced, stored
or transmitted in any form, or by any means, only with the prior permission in writing of the publishers,
or in the case of reprographic reproduction, in accordance with the terms of licences issued by the
Copyright Licensing Agency. Enquiries concerning reproduction outside those terms should be sent to the publishers.

The CD-ROM may not be reproduced for use by others without prior written permission from SAGE. The CD-ROM may not be
distributed or sold separately from the book without the prior written permission of SAGE. All material is © Chris Dukes and
Maggie Smith, 2007

Paul Chapman Publishing
A SAGE Publications Company
1 Oliver's Yard
55 City Road
London EC1Y 1SP

Sage Publication Inc
2455 Teller Road
Thousand Oaks
California 91320

SAGE Publications India Pvt Ltd
B 1/11 Mohan Cooperative Industrial Area
Mathara Road
New Delhi 110 044

SAGE Publications Asia – Pacific Pte Ltd
33 Pekin Street #02-01
Far East Street
Singapore 048763

SWINDON COLLEGE

LEARNING RESOURCE CENTRE

Library of Congress Control Number: 2007934550

British Library Cataloguing in Publication Data

A catalogue record for this book is available from the British Library

ISBN 978-1-4129-4523-3
ISBN 978-1-4129-4524-0 (pbk)

Typeset by Pantek Arts Ltd, Maidstone, Kent
Printed in Great Britain by Cromwell Press Ltd, Trowbridge, Wiltshire
Printed on paper from sustainable resources

Contents

Contents of the CD-ROM

How to use the CD-ROM

The CD-ROM contains pdf files, labelled 'Worksheets.pdf', which contain worksheets from this book. You will need Acrobat Reader version 3 or higher to view and print these pages.

The document is set to print at A4 but you can enlarge them to A3 by increasing the output percentage using the page set-up settings for your printer.

Throughout the book, you will see this CD icon used . This indicates that the material you are looking at is also available electronically on the accompanying CD-ROM.

Contents of the CD-ROM

Acknowledgements

This book is dedicated to all our friends, family and colleagues with whom we have spent many happy hours talking.

To Pammie, with love and thanks, for your friendship, and belief in us.

With thanks also to Jude and Katie at Sage for all their support and encouragement.

Introduction

In our experience pre-school Practitioners want to do the best for the children in their care. They are always looking for practical advice and new ideas. In this Hands-on Guide we aim to assist practitioners in supporting the language and communication of the children in their pre-school.

Each chapter can be used alone for straightforward advice and ideas or quick reference. The book can be read as an overview of language development with guidance to support sound pre-school practice.

In Chapters 2–7 you will be given:

▶ an understanding of the stages of language development 0–5;

▶ an awareness of causes for concern;

▶ ideas on effective and reflective practice;

▶ guidance to make the most of one-on-one moments;

▶ a bank of language-rich activities to use with all children 0–5.

In Chapters 8–10 you will be given an understanding of:

▶ the needs of bilingual children;

▶ specific language-based play activities such as heuristic play, persona dolls and puppets, story sacks and circle time;

▶ planning for individual needs including case studies.

Pre-school practitioners

This book will enable you to develop your knowledge and understanding of pre-school communication and language. You will be supported by practical examples and pro-formas and formats for ideas to use within your setting. These can be used as presented in the book or adapted or personalised to suit your own needs. The hands-on activities will provide a starting point for team discussion.

Tutors and students

Through reading this book you will increase your awareness of the development of children's language and begin to understand and build on your own current and future practice. The Hands-on activities can be used as short assignments.

Advisers

Use this book to support pre-schools to improve their knowledge, understanding and practice in the area of communication and language. Stand-alone chapters can be used as the basis of training. The hands-on activities will provide discussion points for staff teams.

Parents, carers and childminders

This will be a useful introduction to a child's language and communication development. The activities, strategies and ideas are all relevant and can be easily adapted for the home environment.

A note on the text

The case studies included in this publication are a composite of numerous children in various settings, distilled from the authors' many years of experience. They are not specific to any one child, practitioner or setting.

A crossword – words for practitioners

To get you started here is a quick crossword containing words which are explained at various points throughout the book.

Have a go and test your knowledge of some basic terms connected with speech, language and communication.

The solution is provided in Appendix B at the back of the book.

Across

3 The name given to the later stages of babbling involving different sounds and tones which might include the odd real word (6)

10 Communication which does not rely on words (3-6)

11 The production of speech sounds (12)

12 *See 2 down*

13 Exaggerated form of speech and simplified language often used by adults, particularly mothers, to babies and young children (9)

Down

1 Sounds produced before speech development (8)

2 *and* **12** *across*   The way a person uses their body to communicate (4, 8)

4 Showing or demonstrating how to use language (9)

5 How words are articulated or produced (13)

6 The words a child uses (10)

7 Hand gestures that have meaning (7)

8 A word or part of a word that is produced by a single effort of the voice (8)

9 To do with hearing (8)

CHAPTER ONE

Getting started: people, places, play and planning

The aim of this chapter is to show how all aspects of the pre-school environment are relevant to the successful development of children's language and communication. It outlines how to use people, places, play and planning for the benefit of all children in your setting.

The chapter outlines

▶ **People** – the role of the practitioner, 10 key strategies, golden questions and adapting adult-speak

▶ **Places** – creating an environment to support language and communication

▶ **Play** – the Early Years Foundation Stage and language-rich activities

▶ **Planning** – sample pro-forma

People

The role of the practitioner

The ability to communicate well with each other is the most important skill that children will learn. In the pre-school the most important resource is the people. It is vital therefore that they are equipped with the skills and know-how to carry out their role effectively.

The adults, be they practitioner or parent, should be aware of how the quality of *their* language and experiences offered influence a young child's language.

On the following pages and throughout the book there are strategies to support practitioners in recognising and fostering their role as model, sympathetic listener and facilitator of a young child's developing communication and language skills.

Below there is an outline and explanation of '10 Key Strategies for Practitioners', a list of open-ended 'golden questions' and tips on how adults can adjust their language to best meet the needs of all of the children in their care. Through regular use these ideas will become embedded and will improve the early years' practice of those working with babies and young children.

The 10 Key Strategies for Practitioners

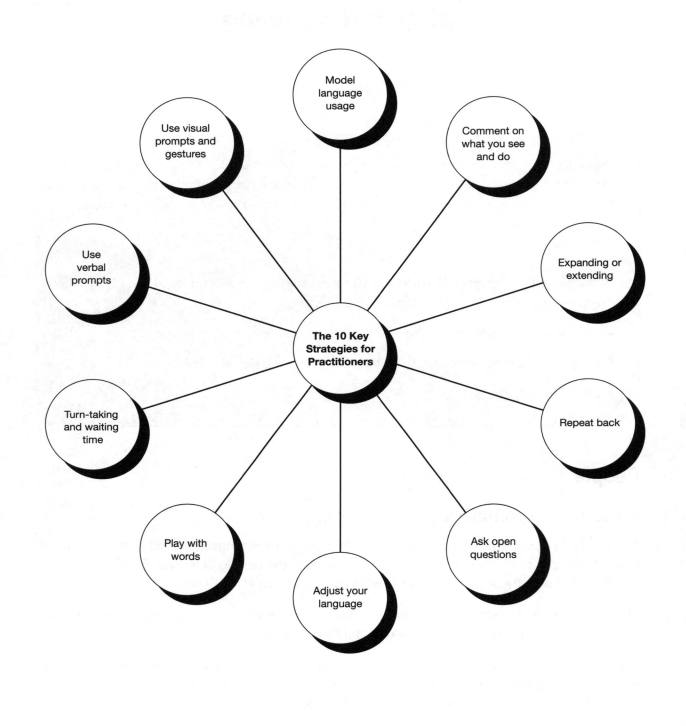

Developing Pre-School Communication and Language, Paul Chapman Publishing © Chris Dukes and Maggie Smith, 2007

The 10 Key Strategies Explained

1. Modelling

This means that the practitioner says the word or phrases that the child wants or needs. In doing so the practitioner 'models' the correct version.

2. Commenting

This means that the practitioner talks about what she or the child is doing as they are doing it, something like a running commentary. This allows the child to hear vocabulary and language in the context of a real situation.

3. Expanding or extending

This is, as it suggests, taking something that the child has said and expanding upon it. So a single word 'Drink' becomes 'You want a drink?' In this way language is modelled and extended to encourage the child to move on to the next step.

4. Repeating back

This means that the practitioner listens to what a child says and then repeats it back to the child, making any necessary corrections without drawing the child's attention to them. This allows the practitioner to check that they have understood what the child has said and also gives the child the satisfaction of hearing their own language acknowledged.

5. Asking open questions

Generally, questioning is best kept to a minimum. When questions are used they should be as open as possible – which is harder than you think! Open-ended questions or *golden questions* have many possible answers and can lead to interesting conversations with young children. (Twenty examples of 'golden questions' to use in your pre-school are given on page 5 below)

6. Playing with words

This means singing songs and saying rhymes but also using spontaneous opportunities to play with words. Children appreciate the sound of words that rhyme, tongue twisters, alliteration or silly sentences, even if they don't fully understand every word.

7. Turn-taking and waiting time

A pause also indicates that you may be waiting for a response and helps to establish the idea of turn-taking which is essential in developing conversation and social skills. Practitioners should try not to rush in when a child hesitates. Many use the three-second rule – when asking a question or seeking a response from a child wait for three seconds before speaking again yourself. This gives the child time to think and compose a response.

8. Using verbal prompts and giving choices

If a child is finding it hard to remember a word or phrase practitioners can prompt them with the first sound of the word or the first couple of words of a phrase. This is often enough to jog the child's memory, allows the child to complete the word or phrase themselves and gives a sense of achievement. Alternatively a child can be given two choices which are modelled to them 'Would you like milk or juice?' In this way the child does not have to think of the word as well as say it.

9. Using visual prompts and gestures

Much of this comes naturally – we often point, pull faces or gesture to enhance or emphasise what we say. Body language also plays a part in conveying meaning. In using these, practitioners can support children's understanding.

10. Adjusting your language

Using simple, less complex sentences at an individual child's level is another way for a practitioner to ensure that they are understood, and of modelling clear language. (See the diagram on 'Adult Speak' below.)

20 Golden Questions

What would happen if …?

I wonder …?

What do you suppose …?

How did that happen …?

What do you think about …?

Tell me about …?

What would you do …?

How can we …?

How did you …?

Tell me about your …?

What else can you do with the …?

How does that feel?

Is there any other way to do this?

Why does it …?

Tell me what it looks like.

Tell me what it sounds like.

What do you think is happening?

How do you do that?

What should we do next?

How does that work?

 Developing Pre-School Communication and Language, Paul Chapman Publishing © Chris Dukes and Maggie Smith, 2007

Adult Speak – Adjusting Your Language

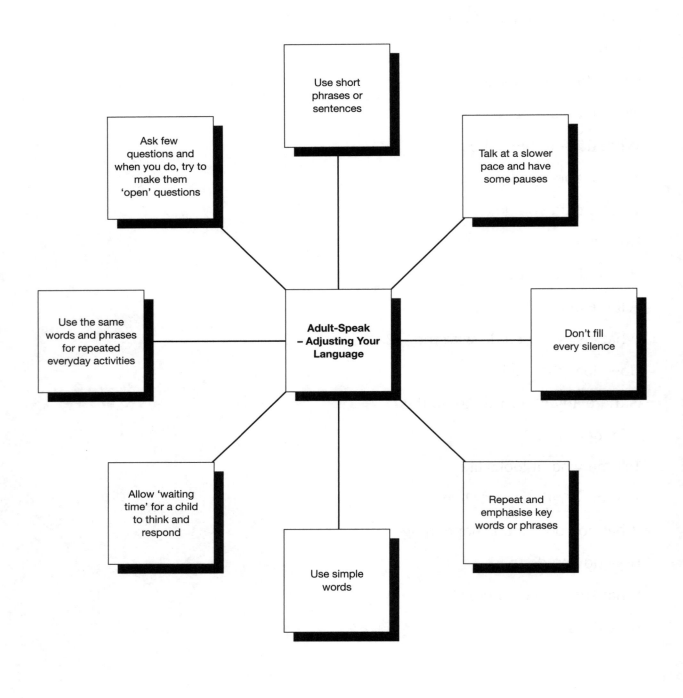

Use short phrases or sentences

Ask few questions and when you do, try to make them 'open' questions

Talk at a slower pace and have some pauses

Use the same words and phrases for repeated everyday activities

Adult-Speak – Adjusting Your Language

Don't fill every silence

Allow 'waiting time' for a child to think and respond

Use simple words

Repeat and emphasise key words or phrases

> ## Top Tip
>
> Pin the golden questions up around the pre-school to remind you of the types of questions to ask.

Places

In addition to practitioners having strategies at their fingertips it is important to create an environment which supports communication and language development. It should be the intention of every practitioner to create a stimulating welcoming, language-rich environment.

Every child, to be educationally successful, needs a language-rich environment, one in which adults speak well, listen attentively, and read aloud every day. (Boyer, 1991)

Below are some ideas to help you achieve this.

Creating an Environment to Support Speech and Language Development

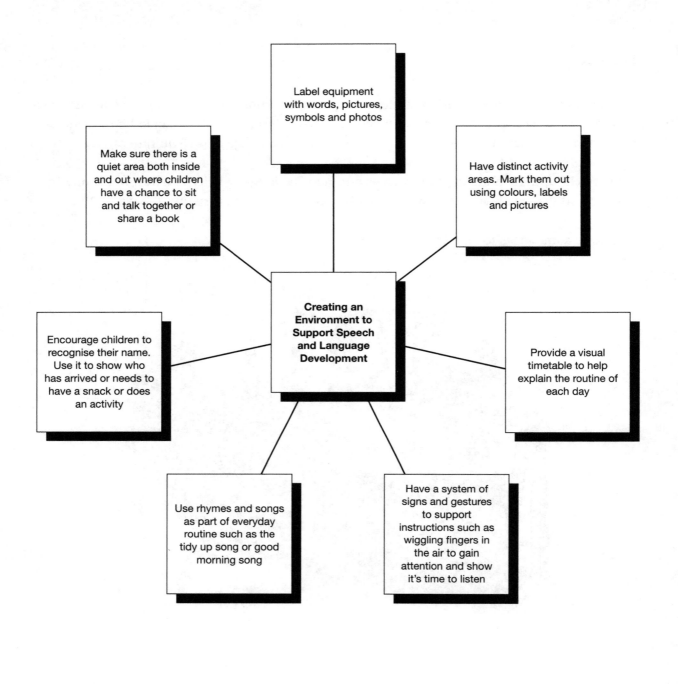

Label equipment with words, pictures, symbols and photos

Make sure there is a quiet area both inside and out where children have a chance to sit and talk together or share a book

Have distinct activity areas. Mark them out using colours, labels and pictures

Creating an Environment to Support Speech and Language Development

Encourage children to recognise their name. Use it to show who has arrived or needs to have a snack or does an activity

Provide a visual timetable to help explain the routine of each day

Use rhymes and songs as part of everyday routine such as the tidy up song or good morning song

Have a system of signs and gestures to support instructions such as wiggling fingers in the air to gain attention and show it's time to listen

Developing Pre-School Communication and Language, Paul Chapman Publishing © Chris Dukes and Maggie Smith, 2007

Play

All pre-schools offer countless language opportunities for their babies and children. Practitioners who offer a wide and varied curriculum can be assured that they are meeting the language needs of most of the children who attend the setting.

By becoming aware of how much language permeates the whole early years curriculum practitioners can develop an inbuilt ability to make the most of the language potential of *any* pre-school activity.

The Early Years Foundation Stage recognises that children learn holistically, that is they learn lots of things at the same time in their own unique way. It follows then that specific language activities need not be the only way to develop a child's language and communication skills.

The key to providing a language-rich curriculum is to make the most of every learning opportunity. Through regular practice practitioners can develop the skills needed to turn every activity into a language opportunity.

All early years practitioners know that children and babies are learning all sorts of things all of the time. Children do not define their learning by curriculum headings. None of the six areas of learning can be delivered in isolation from the others – each is equally important and dependent on the others.

Examples of language-rich curriculum activities can be found at the end of each of Chapters 2–7. The activities outlined – and indeed all pre-school activities – can be enhanced by using the planning sheets outlined below. These will be particularly helpful when planning for children who may need additional support in developing their communication and language skills.

Planning

Below you will find a 'Speech and Language Activity Planner' pro forma and a sample completed planner. This can be useful for:

▶ analysing activities to make the most of their language content;

▶ planning for developing specific language skills;

▶ planning for individuals who may need extra input or those who have an IEP (Individual Education Plan).

It is recognised that practitioners spend a great deal of time on their planning. Through planning practitioners learn to embed good practice into their everyday work. We would suggest that the Speech and Language Activity Planner is used as a tool to develop practitioners' own skills and to help them reflect on their choice of activities.

Speech and Language Activity Planner

Touch Tour

	Notes
Target child / children Language possibilities and objectives ᐅ New keywords ᐅ Language to model ᐅ Will listening skills be developed? ᐅ When will this happen?	

Points to remember:

ᐅ

ᐅ

How the activity went and what was noticed/next steps

 Developing Pre-School Communication and Language, Paul Chapman Publishing © Chris Dukes and Maggie Smith, 2007

Sample Completed Planner
Speech and Language Activity Planner

Touch Tour

Target child / children With Sam

Language possibilities and objectives

▷ New keywords

   window, garden, trees, flowers

▷ Language to model

   'through the window'

   'on the grass'

   'beautiful flowers'

▷ Will listening skills be developed?

   Yes. Throughout the tour, I will look at Sam's face and wait for a response.

▷ When will this happen?

   Throughout the activity.

Notes

Ask Mum for some key words in home language to use with Sam

Sam seems to listen intently to my voice, he responds by cooing and smiling

Points to remember:

▷ Dress up Sam warmly when going outside as he is susceptible to the cold weather

▷ Write down the French words given to me by Sam's Mum for future use

How the activity went and what was noticed/next steps

Sam seemed to repeat some of the words I was using especially 'grass' and 'window'. Remember to tell his Mum and put on records. Sam bounced up and down when I used the French words!

Developing Pre-School Communication and Language, Paul Chapman Publishing © Chris Dukes and Maggie Smith, 2007

Further reading

Dukes, C. and Smith, M. (2006) *A Practical Guide to Pre-school Inclusion*, Hands-on Guides Series. Paul Chapman Publishing.

Tassoni, P. (2005) *Planning, Play and the Early Years*. Harcourt Heinemann.

Whitehead, M. R. (2007) *Developing Language and Literacy with Young Children*, 3rd edn, 0–8 Series. Paul Chapman Publishing.

CHAPTER TWO

BABIES: 0–11 MONTHS

In this chapter you will find:

▶ An overview of language development

▶ Appropriate expectations for children's development

▶ An outline of effective and reflective early years practice

▶ How to make the most of one-on-one moments

▶ Curriculum-based language-rich activities

▶ A hands-on activity

Overview: 0–11 months

Babies are born with a desire to communicate and already possess some of the skills to do so. Babies learn about their world through their senses and so sight, touch and sound are key to developing these early skills. Through crying, body movements and eye contact they look for responses and want to interact with those closest to them.

Newborn babies communicate much of the time through crying. Having a key person who gets to know each baby well is vitally important, especially in these very early days. The close bond that develops is vital for the baby's sense of well-being. This in turn will enable the baby to thrive and learn.

An experienced practitioner will soon learn to differentiate between the cry that says 'I'm hungry' and the cry that says 'My nappy needs to be changed', in much the same way as parents do.

There are other less obvious ways that a baby will begin to communicate with those around them. Babies can differentiate between the sound of a human voice and other sounds. They will already associate a specific voice or a tone of voice with care, food and warmth. Babies may respond to a familiar voice by appearing calm and quiet or by waving their arms and legs around.

Babies will learn the ways in which adults communicate with them through holding, cuddling, touching and making facial gestures. Some babies find comfort in motion, such as rocking or walking back and forth, while others need soft singing or other familiar noises when they are upset. Each baby will respond in their own unique way.

Gradually babies are able to focus more clearly and can very soon recognise a human face and especially those of familiar carers. Touch and hearing remain especially important, however. It is never too early to start talking to a baby because even though they do not understand the words, the sound and tone of your words will reassure them and make them feel safe. All of these experiences and moments together help to create a bond between adult and child which is the beginning of learning about communication.

Babies can hear from inside their mother's womb even before birth, so talking and listening to babies from the moment they are born helps them to develop good language and communication skills.

Understanding 0–11 Months: Appropriate Expectations

Watches your face with interest when you talk

Begins to recognise main carer's voice

Is startled by sudden or loud noises

Beginning to understand

Recognises familiar faces and objects

Is soothed by calm or gentle voices or music

Responds to name – will turn head towards carer

Follows moving objects with eyes

Remember all children are different – some will exceed these expectations while others will be on their way to achieving them.

Developing Pre-School Communication and Language, Paul Chapman Publishing © Chris Dukes and Maggie Smith, 2007

Expressing 0–11 months: appropriate expectations

▶ *Tries* to 'talk' to you using gesture and sound

▶ *Smiles* at people

▶ *Cries*, gurgle, grunts and coos, to self and others

▶ *Uses* a special cry when hungry

▶ *Begins* to laugh and squeal with delight

▶ *Reaches* or moves towards toys or desired objects

▶ *Coos* or squeals for attention

▶ *Complains* or pulls faces

▶ *Babbles* single syllable sounds, e.g. da da, ba ba, ma ma

▶ *Begins* to imitate some sounds

What to look out for

▶ A baby who does not smile

▶ A baby who does not cry to express hunger or pain

▶ A baby who does not turn their head towards a voice or sound

▶ A baby who makes no attempt to vocalise or babble

▶ A baby who does not follow a moving object with their eyes

▶ A baby who is not interested in interacting with their carer through games like peek-a-boo

Effective Practice 0–11 Months

Ideas to introduce or consolidate

Although it is unusual to have newborn babies in the pre-school, increasingly some pre-schools are admitting babies as young as three or four months. Many practitioners spend some time during their careers working in a home situation as nannies or childminders.

Even the youngest babies are learning how to communicate. The more you listen and respond to babies, the better they will become at communicating with others in the world around them.

Imitation

This is one of the best strategies that babies have. They look directly at an adult's face with an open gaze and are ready for communication to take place. It is estimated that at only three days old babies tune in and recognise their mother's voice. In the same way they will attune themselves to their carer's voice.

Practitioners are providing a useful role model for babies even at such a young age.

The patterns and intonations of the human voice are quickly picked up by the youngest of babies. Adults need to talk to and look directly at babies showing them how to communicate effectively. If a baby babbles count these sounds as a conversation – coo or talk back, imitating the sing-song of a baby's rhythms.

Most practitioners instinctively use 'Motherese' when engaging with infants. This is the sing-song voice often used by adults when talking to babies. Using this type of voice holds the baby's attention and allows productive communication to develop. When talking to a baby, pause and allow time for the baby to respond: in that way a conversation is taking place and the practitioners is actually teaching the baby about the conventions of human speech – listening and contributing.

Babies need to learn the symbolic meaning of words and practitioners are well placed to help babies learn words and classify their world. When babies point, practitioners need to tell the baby simply the name of the object they are pointing at. Similarly the practitioners begin to label the babies' world for them by simply putting a name or sound to all of those objects the baby comes into contact with. Eventually the practitioner will begin to hear an echo as the baby learns to imitate speech and words.

Looking

Practitioners need to hold the gaze of an adoring baby. In doing this they are reaffirming that the baby is important and that the practitioner is interested in and concerned for their needs.

Babies use their eyes to get messages across. They often point with their eyes to what they want. An observant practitioner often can instantly know what a baby wants or needs. Sometimes this is instinct but often it is because the practitioner is watching the baby and can tell what they need. A tuned-in practitioner takes away frustrating attempts by a baby to make their carer understand what they want. There is, however, a fine line to be drawn between anticipating needs and taking away the baby's need to communicate.

Listening

Crying is a baby's insurance policy that it will not be ignored by the world. Different cries have different meanings. Practitioners need to listen to a baby to learn to understand what the different sounds and cries mean. Sometimes a baby wants to be fed or is uncomfortable, perhaps in a soiled nappy. Often they just want to get the attention and company of the adults around them.

Babbling is a baby experimenting with speech and sound, patterns and often is not a sign of distress. It is in fact a workout for the vocal cords. Babbling is often an invitation to the practitioner to come and have a chat.

Once practitioners begin to listen carefully to baby's sounds, they will quickly come to recognise the baby's own unique language. Babbling will become more varied and begin to resemble the child's mother tongue and eventually the practitioner will be rewarded with sounds that begin to have meaning. By the time a baby reaches the end of their first year they may be on the brink of speaking.

> **Although most infants do not learn to talk until their second year, their voices are there for us to hear from birth.** (*Rouse Selleck, 1995*)

Making the Most of one-on-one Moments: 0–11 Months

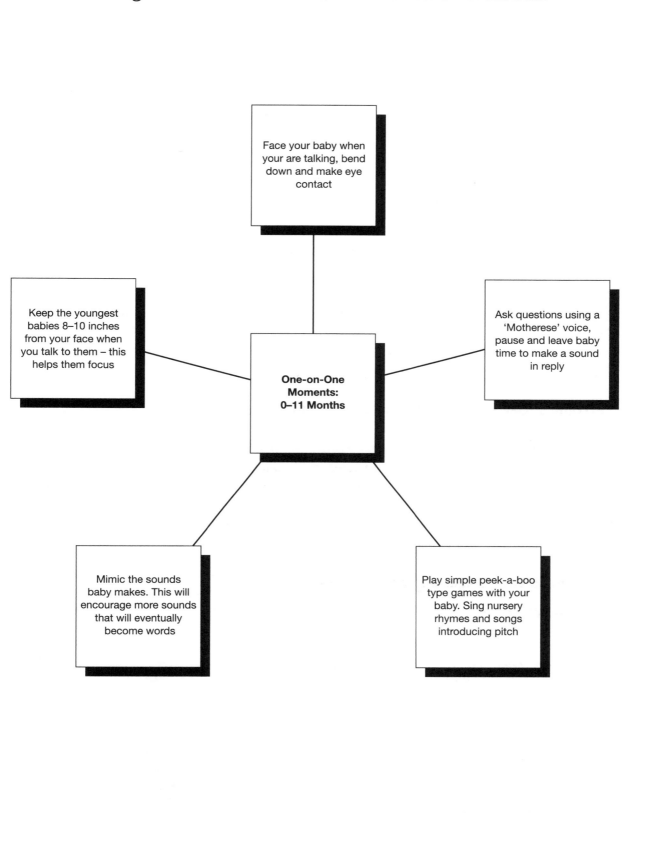

Face your baby when your are talking, bend down and make eye contact

Keep the youngest babies 8–10 inches from your face when you talk to them – this helps them focus

Ask questions using a 'Motherese' voice, pause and leave baby time to make a sound in reply

One-on-One Moments: 0–11 Months

Mimic the sounds baby makes. This will encourage more sounds that will eventually become words

Play simple peek-a-boo type games with your baby. Sing nursery rhymes and songs introducing pitch

 Developing Pre-School Communication and Language, Paul Chapman Publishing © Chris Dukes and Maggie Smith, 2007

Activities for a language-rich pre-school: 0–11 months

Physical development

On a roll

Babies learn to roll over on their own and don't need to be taught, but you can help to strengthen the muscles involved by laying the baby on his or her side and providing support from behind with a rolled up blanket.

Lie down adjacent to the baby and encourage reaching for you. Eventually, he or she will topple forward and then be able to do so with intention. Encourage repetitions with a favourite toy or by smiling and talking, using encouraging phrases like 'come on, you can do it', 'brilliant, you clever boy/girl' etc.

Knowledge and understanding of the world

Touch Tour

Give babies a bird's eye view of their world. Carry a baby around at your eye level and name each object as you touch it. Include things like windows, doors, toys, books and other adults and other babies. This game can also be carried outdoors. When the baby is older, include touching for the baby too (see the sample planning sheet in Chapter 1).

Personal social and emotional development

Early conversation

Babies are fascinated with faces and voices, and your first communications are through the sounds you make and the nearness of your face. Get up close and personal with babies, look into their eyes and chatter away (the content need not be earth shattering!), tell them what you are doing and where you are going etc. Pause and allow the baby time to respond by making a sound. Show pleasure and delight when the baby talks back to you.

Problem-solving, reasoning and numeracy

Find the ticking clock

Buy a large ticking alarm clock. Show the ticking clock to the baby letting him or her explore and touch it. Put the clock under a blanket on the floor and let the baby roll or crawl around looking for the clock. Shower the baby with praise when he or she finds the clock. Make the game harder by putting it in a shoe box etc. This game can also be carried out with musical toys.

Creative development

Bubble catch

Make or buy bubbles. With babies sitting in highchairs, or propped up with cushions, blow bubbles in the babies' direction (avoiding their faces). Encourage babies to watch, clap and catch the bubbles. Hold a large bubble on the wand and let the baby look at it closely. Encourage the baby to pop the bubble when he or she has finished looking. Remember to comment on what you are doing.

Note: Make sure you have a washing cloth on hand to wipe baby's hands after the activity.

Communication, language and literacy

Body parts

Get a small special sample piece of material. During *one-on-one* time with a baby use the material to teach body part names. Put the material on your head saying 'my head', then put it on the baby's head saying 'your head' and continue with other body parts, touching your nose, ears, etc. then the baby's with the material. This will soon turn into a fun time and will often end up as a peek-a-boo type game.

 Hands-on activity

There has been a lot of focus lately on signing with babies. Signing used alongside speech has been shown to increase a baby's ability to develop its language skills.

Using the following internet links see if you can find out more about how to do this. Take your research and findings back to your staff team for an interesting discussion.

▶ www.babysigners.co.uk
▶ www.makaton.org/training/baby-signing

 Further reading

Meggit, C. (2006) *Child Development: An Illustrated Guide*, 2nd edn. Heinemann.
Sheridan, M. D., Frost, M. and Sharma, A. (1997) *From Birth to Five Years: Children's Developmental Progress*, revised edn. Routledge.

CHAPTER THREE

 # Babies and toddlers: 8–20 months

In this chapter you will find:

▶ An overview of language development

▶ Appropriate expectations for children's development

▶ An outline of effective and reflective early years practice

▶ How to make the most of one-on-one moments

▶ Curriculum-based language-rich activities

▶ A hands-on activity.

Overview: 8–20 months

Over the first year babies gradually begin to widen their horizons. They begin to listen and interact with sounds, objects and people other than their caregiver. They will begin to recognise words in speech and to show an interest in noisy toys and music. Increasingly babies develop links between words and their meanings as they become able to follow a pointing finger or direct their gaze at an object. It is therefore very important that adults support the building of these links by showing and naming everyday objects, talking through daily routines and introducing the baby to new experiences.

Gradually babies will learn that certain familiar objects have certain uses and will be able to point at or fetch these objects. Through play and exploration babies will also come to recognise similarities and differences and will begin to realise that objects have different properties. Much of this experience is gained through exploring with their mouth as well as engaging in repetitive play guided by an adult.

Familiar actions and associated words are also learnt through everyday routines of eating and drinking or nappy changing as well as those associated with rhymes and games such as tickling or bouncing, sliding or swinging.

Gesture also develops throughout this stage with nodding, waving goodbye or holding up arms to indicate that they want to be picked up. A baby at this stage is learning that communication can affect the actions of those around it and is also a way of indicating needs or wants.

Also during these months babbling continues with an increased range of sounds. It develops into what is commonly referred to as jargon. Jargon is quite long babbling which has a combination of sounds and intonations which often sound as if the baby is speaking in sentences.

By about 12 months actual words may be recognisable among babbling and jargon. Pronunciation of words, however, is not fixed and words can be spoken differently each time they are said.

> **A child's first word has behind it a history of listening, observing and experimenting with sounds and highly selective imitations of people.**
> *(Whitehead, 2002)*

Understanding 8–20 Months: Appropriate Expectations

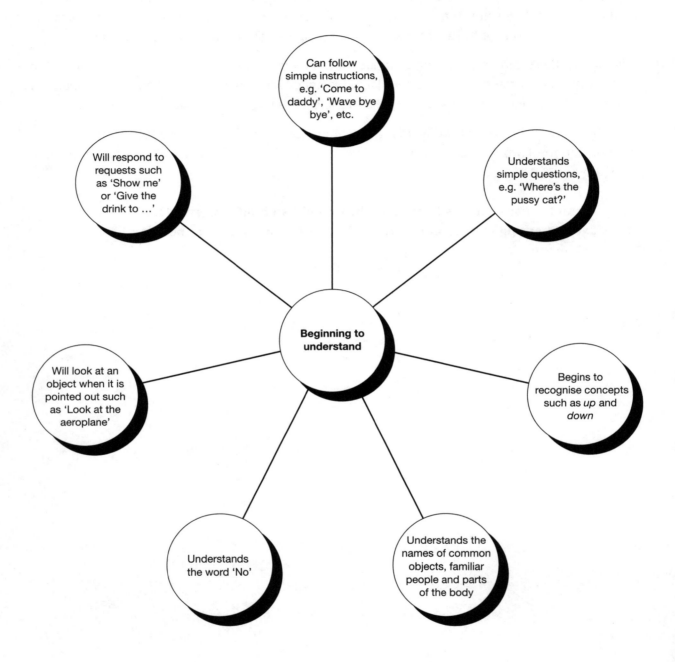

Can follow simple instructions, e.g. 'Come to daddy', 'Wave bye bye', etc.

Will respond to requests such as 'Show me' or 'Give the drink to …'

Understands simple questions, e.g. 'Where's the pussy cat?'

Beginning to understand

Will look at an object when it is pointed out such as 'Look at the aeroplane'

Begins to recognise concepts such as *up* and *down*

Understands the word 'No'

Understands the names of common objects, familiar people and parts of the body

Remember, all children are different – some will exceed these expectations while others will be on their way to achieving them.

Developing Pre-School Communication and Language, Paul Chapman Publishing © Chris Dukes and Maggie Smith, 2007

Expressing 8–20 months: appropriate expectations

▶ Continues to imitate sounds

▶ Begins joining sounds to sound like words (jargoning)

▶ Learns to say first real words, usually animals or everyday objects

▶ Repeats words said by adults (echolalia)

▶ Acquires 1–3 words per month

▶ Uses the same word to identify similar objects, e.g. all animals may be called 'cats', all round objects are 'balls', etc. (This is to overextend or holophrase.)

▶ Uses language to gain information by beginning to ask simple questions

▶ Begins to use different tones of voice

▶ Begins to join in with simple action rhymes

▶ Will indicate needs by pointing, gestures and words

▶ Will refer to themselves by name

▶ Will begin to speak up to 30/40 words and understand many more

What to look out for

▶ Does not turn towards a voice that calls their name

▶ Does not produce lots of noises and babble

▶ Does not look in the direction of a pointing finger

▶ Has little interest in what is going on around them

▶ Dislikes body contact

▶ Demands little attention and no has no interest in playing

▶ Has no single words by 16 months

▶ Stops using words

Effective Practice 8–20 Months

Ideas to introduce or consolidate

First words

The first words taught to a child should reflect the events, routines and objects that are already familiar to him/her. Early words should be as short as possible and be general in their reference, e.g. 'dog' instead of a type of dog like 'poodle'. These general reference words can be learned and remembered more easily by young children. They are also more useful to children as by using them, they can have their meaning easily understood by other children as well as adults.

Practitioners should get into the habit of naming objects, actions and events to children throughout the day. However, although practitioners need to talk to children by constantly providing a running commentary on events, they must be careful to leave spaces and provide encouragement for children to express themselves. Children need to be provided with a safe environment where they can practise the use of their voice.

Practice makes perfect

Practitioners can encourage the use of spoken language by children in a variety of fun ways. Simple action songs should be part of the everyday curriculum – by using actions, toys or real objects practitioners reinforce object names and actions. Simple action songs such as 'this is the way you brush your teeth', 'comb your hair' 'put on your shoes' etc. teach both the names of everyday objects and provide the matching action.

Pretend play such as tea parties, bathing dolls and reading stories to teddy all provide children with a worthwhile opportunity to practise and learn new language skills. The language being spoken could range from naming body parts to the language of feelings and empathy.

Using a child's special interest or favourite types of activities is often the best motivator to language and communication. This means that practitioners need to take the time to observe children, talk to parents and find out what children really like to do.

Top Tip

Remember the use of natural gestures to support your language with young children, or learn the Makaton signs for some key words. This will go far to support any child's acquisition of words and meaning.

There are some commercially available videos that teach practitioners how to do this.

Building confidence

By talking and listening with young children, the adults around them provide them with the growing confidence they need to become effective communicators. By allowing a child the space and opportunity to communicate, as well as providing a good role model for effective communication, practitioners create a perfect environment for communication to blossom.

Effective practitioners allow children opportunities for repetition and mistakes, as well as the golden silence often needed for a child to find just the right word they need to express themselves.

In those environments where the adults communicate acceptance and always try to validate a child's right to be heard the children are far more likely to share their emerging ideas and feelings. By offering small groups for activities, one-on-one opportunities together with a calm and stimulating atmosphere, practitioners will provide young children with the desire to exchange ideas and feelings with those around them.

Young children communicate because they want to. The main role of the practitioner is to allow them the time and space to do this.

Making the Most of One-on-One Moments: 8–20 Months

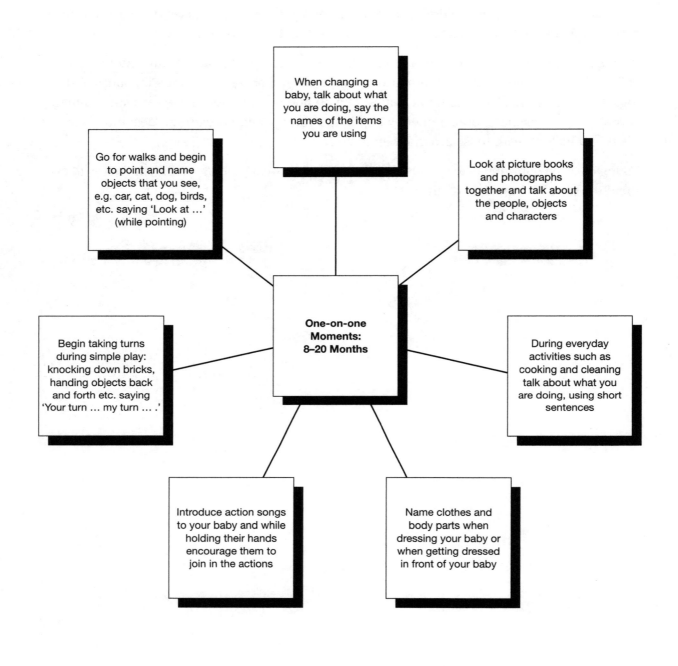

When changing a baby, talk about what you are doing, say the names of the items you are using

Go for walks and begin to point and name objects that you see, e.g. car, cat, dog, birds, etc. saying 'Look at …' (while pointing)

Look at picture books and photographs together and talk about the people, objects and characters

Begin taking turns during simple play: knocking down bricks, handing objects back and forth etc. saying 'Your turn … my turn … .'

One-on-one Moments: 8–20 Months

During everyday activities such as cooking and cleaning talk about what you are doing, using short sentences

Introduce action songs to your baby and while holding their hands encourage them to join in the actions

Name clothes and body parts when dressing your baby or when getting dressed in front of your baby

Developing Pre-School Communication and Language, Paul Chapman Publishing © Chris Dukes and Maggie Smith, 2007

Activities for a language-rich pre-school: 8–20 months

Physical development

Reaching out

Using a baby gym, play mat or favourite toy, play with the baby, exploring the possibilities of the equipment. Lay out a selection of the toys around the floor on a mat. Lie down with the baby and play a stretching and rolling game with them as they reach out to get a favourite toy. Encourage the baby to reach out for themselves but be on hand in case they cannot reach. Comment on the activity saying things like 'Ah, you want the teddy – reach out your arm' etc.

Knowledge and understanding of the world

Exploration walks (can also be carried out in a pre-school garden)

Go out walking or take a turn around the nursery garden with the baby either being carried or in a pushchair or with baby toddling. Walk slowly, stopping and drawing the baby's attention to details such as trees, flowers, birds, etc. Lift up any stones or logs and with the baby look at what is underneath. Look over fences, under benches and into the sky. Point and show and tell the baby all you see.

Personal social and emotional development

Looking after each other bag

Put together a small bag with items that are used to 'look after each other', e.g. a soft brush, a face cloth, a toothbrush, an empty pot of baby cream, etc. Encourage the baby to pull something out of the bag and say 'Look a hairbrush, brush your hair', then show the baby how to do this. Then develop the activity to encourage the baby to brush your hair saying 'That's lovely, you are looking after me' etc. This will help the baby to develop empathy as well as learn new words. This activity can be carried out with a baby and an older child, with the practitioner modelling how to look after each other.

Note: When using pots of baby cream make sure the pots are empty and pretend to be using the cream. This will also help develop imaginative or pretend play.

Problem-solving, reasoning and numeracy

Digging for treasure

Hide objects and toys (not too small) underneath or in a pile of scrunched up magazines or wrapping paper either piled up on the floor or in a box. With the baby begin to remove the newspapers to find the hidden treasure. Say 'Look, a …' Encourage the baby to crawl around looking for more objects. Join in enthusiastically.

Tip: Keep the scrunched up papers for future activities.

Creative development

Messy finger painting

Using a selection of small squeezy paint bottles ask the toddler to choose a colour of paint. Help them squeeze some onto a tray with deep edges. Encourage the toddler to put his or her hands into the paint, feeling and mixing it. Encourage the toddler to use his or her fingers as a paint brush and draw circles and swirls in the tray. The practitioner can at this point help the toddler to take a print by placing a piece of paper on top of the paint and slowly peeling it off. But remember the activity is about the 'doing' and not the end product. Comment on how the paint feels, copying words or sounds the toddler makes.

Note: Always have a basin of soapy water and a cloth ready to wash the toddler's hands. (This often turns into another activity in itself!)

Communication, language and literacy

Finger rhymes and nursery rhymes

Babies of this age are beginning to join in and get excited about songs and music. Choose a few finger rhymes to sing regularly to babies and toddlers, and show them the actions by moving their arms or demonstrating the moves in front of them. Choose repetitive and short songs and sing them regularly, such as 'Round and Round the Garden', 'Two Little Dickie Birds' 'Five Fat Sausages', etc. Buy a good book which contains lots of nursery rhymes and songs as well as finger rhymes for practitioners to use. Regularly have music with nursery rhymes playing in the pre-school. Singing is a good way to practise 'finding your voice'

Hands-on activity

In a staff meeting begin to compile a list of simple action songs to sing with a baby/toddler. Choose short songs that have words that the child can pick up easily. Look for pictures and props that can be used to illustrate the meaning of the songs and nursery rhymes.

Here are some to get you started:

▶ *Two Little Dicky Birds*

▶ *Round and Round the Garden Like a Teddy Bear*

▶ *This Little Piggy Went to Market*

 Further reading

Meggitt, C. (2006) *Child Development: An Illustrated Guide*, 2nd edn. Heinemann.
Sheridan, M. D., Frost, M. and Sharma, A. (1997) *From Birth to Five Years: Children's Developmental Progress*, revised edn. Routledge.

CHAPTER FOUR

Toddlers: 16–26 months

In this chapter you will find:

▶ An overview of language development

▶ Appropriate expectations for children's development

▶ An outline of effective and reflective early years practice

▶ How to make the most of one-on-one moments

▶ Curriculum-based language-rich activities

▶ A hands-on activity

Overview: 16–24 months

This is the time between infancy and early childhood. The young child's curiosity seems insatiable as they continually talk and babble to themselves and ask the names of objects to anyone around. They then repeat the named object to themselves, sometimes over and over again.

Their own needs are very important to them and they often make these known to others by shouting, pointing or using simple words.

Young children struggle towards independence as they begin to explore their environment and experience a wide variety of emotions such as satisfaction and joy as well as anger and frustration.

One of the greatest pleasures for both practitioners and parents is watching a child's sense of self develop as youngsters begin to define themselves as separate people who want to do things for themselves. They begin to have their own ideas about how things should happen, especially in relation to their care. They can also be vocal and noisy in putting their point of view forward, and practitioners and parents begin to hear the word 'no' many times each day.

These are exciting days and young children are learning fast. They look to the adults around them for help in interpreting the world. As practitioners we should be looking to turn every moment of the day into a learning experience and an opportunity to help young children develop their communication and language skills.

Understanding 16–26 Months: Appropriate Expectations

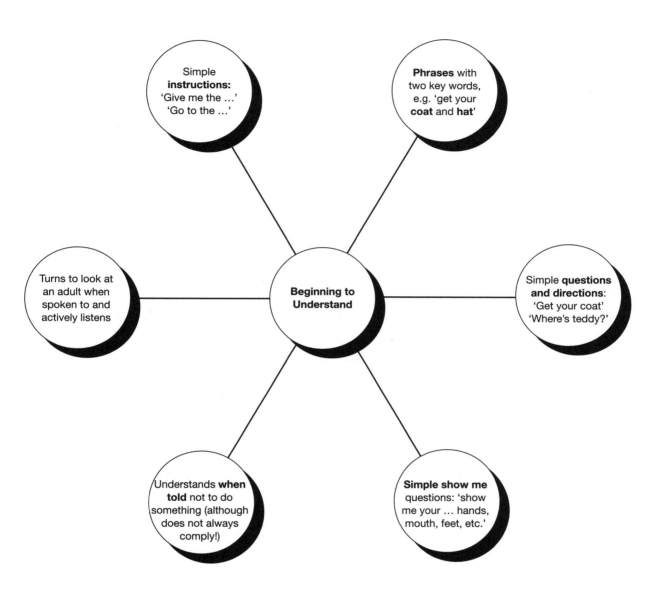

Simple **instructions:** 'Give me the …' 'Go to the …'

Phrases with two key words, e.g. 'get your **coat** and **hat**'

Turns to look at an adult when spoken to and actively listens

Beginning to Understand

Simple **questions and directions:** 'Get your coat' 'Where's teddy?'

Understands **when told** not to do something (although does not always comply!)

Simple show me questions: 'show me your … hands, mouth, feet, etc.'

Remember, all children are different – some will exceed these expectations while others will be on their way to achieving them.

Developing Pre-School Communication and Language, Paul Chapman Publishing © Chris Dukes and Maggie Smith, 2007

Expressing 16–26 months: appropriate expectations

▶ Mutters and talks to self when engaged in activity

▶ Spontaneously uses between 50 and 200 words (or more)

▶ Tries to use words that may not yet be clear

▶ Can say 'no' and begins to show possession, e.g. 'mine'

▶ Can ask for what they want using words or gestures, pointing, saying 'uhuh' or 'mama'

▶ Puts simple words and gestures together, e.g. 'whatssat?' while pointing, 'me me' when talking with outstretched arms

▶ Enjoys singing and will attempt to join in

▶ Asks for specific things by name, e.g. 'milk' or 'juice', 'biscuit', etc.

▶ Hands over and names familiar objects and toys on request

▶ Can copy and produce animal sounds, e.g. 'moo' for cow, 'bow bow' for dog, etc.

▶ Begins to combine to words into meaningful phrases such as 'Bye bye Mama'

▶ Begins to use some describing words such as 'big', 'cold', 'hungry'

▶ Begins to ask simple questions: 'Where Daddy?' 'Home now?' 'What's that?'

▶ Repeats adults (echolalia), especially the last word in a sentence before absorbing the new word into his or her own vocabulary

▶ Uses telegraphic speech, e.g. two- or three-word sentences such as 'Mummy car' which could have a variety of different meanings, including 'Mummy's in the car', 'I want to go in the car', etc.

▶ Rapidly introduces new words into their vocabulary

▶ Is able to make his or her own needs known through simple words and gestures e.g. pulls adult by hand, points or uses words like 'more juice'

▶ Begins to listen with some interest to more general talk

▶ Says some two-word sentences such as 'all gone', 'me go', 'more juice', etc.

What to look out for

▶ A child using more gestures than words

▶ Not putting, or beginning to put, two words together

▶ Not wanting to join other children's play

▶ Does not understand words for everyday objects

▶ Does not imitate everyday actions

▶ Unable to concentrate for very short periods on activities they have chosen

Effective Practice 16–26 Months

Ideas to introduce or consolidate

I know what I want

At this age young children know what they mean; however, they often find it difficult to make the adults around them understand. This can lead to frustration. Practitioners should encourage young children to make their needs known. This can be done through a variety of means, e.g. be aware when children point either with their fingers or their eyes. Lift objects, say 'Is this what you want?', and name the objects (thus increasing a child's vocabulary).

Allow children to take your hand and physically show you what they want. Say 'Here, take my hand and show me'.

Although practitioners should make every effort to understand young children and should use a variety of methods to try to understand them, it is worth noting that children should be encouraged to ask or show. Many good practitioners begin to anticipate a child's every need and this often means the child does not get an opportunity to practise language skills. Encourage children to initiate and ask for help – careful prompting and encouragement helps ease the frustration of not being understood.

Getting along together

Learning how to get along and make friends is one of life's most important lessons. Adults play a crucial part not only as role models but also in teaching children the language they need to make positive relationships. Sometimes this language has to be explicitly taught to children through demonstration, e.g. showing children how to share or join in with a game by asking 'Can I play?' or 'Can I have a turn?' Children turn-taking and getting along together make for a happy pre-school.

Parents can be encouraged to further develop these skills at home. Practitioners should inform parents who their child has been playing with and whose company they enjoy.

Emotions and feelings

Children often have strong feelings and can be good at showing emotions in ways such as crying, covering their face and even through tantrums. In order to best express themselves and their wants and needs, children need to learn the language of feelings and emotions. This is a good age for practitioners to introduce concepts such as happy and sad.

Through the use of photographs and picture books, practitioners can begin to help children find the words they themselves need both to express their own feelings and also to begin to understand the feelings of others.

While looking at photographs or picture books practitioners could ask questions like 'Do you think he is sad?' or make comments throughout the day like 'This makes me feel happy'. Make sure non-verbal communication and facial expressions accompany these sessions as some children may not yet understand the words but they will be able to identify with the facial expressions.

What's that for?

Children of this age need to begin to hear more than the symbolic names of objects, e.g. more than an object name, but also a brief description of the function of the object. Practitioners can help children develop this skill through role modelling, e.g. 'Yes a brush – for brushing my hair', 'Your cup – for having a nice drink', 'Your hat – to keep your head nice and warm'. If children see and hear practitioners use this skill they will attempt to copy and develop their own descriptive language.

Making choices

As children's confidence with language and communication grows, practitioners should encourage children to begin to make choices and develop vocabulary. An important part of the development of a child's personality is beginning to make small decisions and learning to compromise. In order to do this a child needs to develop both social skills and vocabulary. Support a child making choices simply by offering choices as often as possible.

Looking and saying

Encourage children to increase vocabulary and begin to become aware of the world around them by modelling observational skills. Develop the habit when you are with the children of looking and saying, or looking and pointing, e.g. when outside with children say 'Look quickly, a cat' or 'Look, a bird in the tree', etc. Accompany your vocalisation with gesture and pointing, get down to the child's level and point to the place you mean. Children will soon catch on to this skill and may begin pointing and pulling you when they see something interesting. Expand by describing what the child points out to you, e.g. if the child says 'cat' expand on the sentence by saying 'Oh yes, a cat in the garden'.

Getting to know each other

The relationship with the practitioner often begins to change as a child's personality and language skills develop. Both practitioners and children begin to question each other and find out more about each other's needs, likes and dislikes. Children will begin to express opinions about what they do and do not like or want, and practitioners need to begin asking questions such as 'Which one would you like?' and 'What will we do now?' Practitioners who work with children of this age sometimes feel that this is the age when a real bond develops between themselves and children, and purposeful interactions are often a mark of this closeness.

Showing and telling

Children are often very excited about showing their own toys, photographs, books and other things from home. By encouraging a 'show and tell' time in your setting practitioners are showing children that they value them and are interested in what they have to say. Children will often be excited to share their toys or experiences within the pre-school. These sessions offer an opportunity to develop vocabulary and consolidate language experiences. Children are seen to grow in confidence when describing or showing their favourite objects while practitioners are provided with an opportunity to build on a child's interest. With such young children these sessions should be short and frequent as the children's interest will wane if they are left for a long time waiting for their turn.

Widening horizons

Practitioners should always strive to offer new and interesting experiences to children. These should include visits, trips and walks. All new experiences offer the opportunity to hear and learn new vocabulary and to widen horizons.

> **The acquisition of a first language is the most complex skill anyone ever learns.** *(Crystal, 1987)*

Making the Most of One-on-One Moments: 16–26 Months

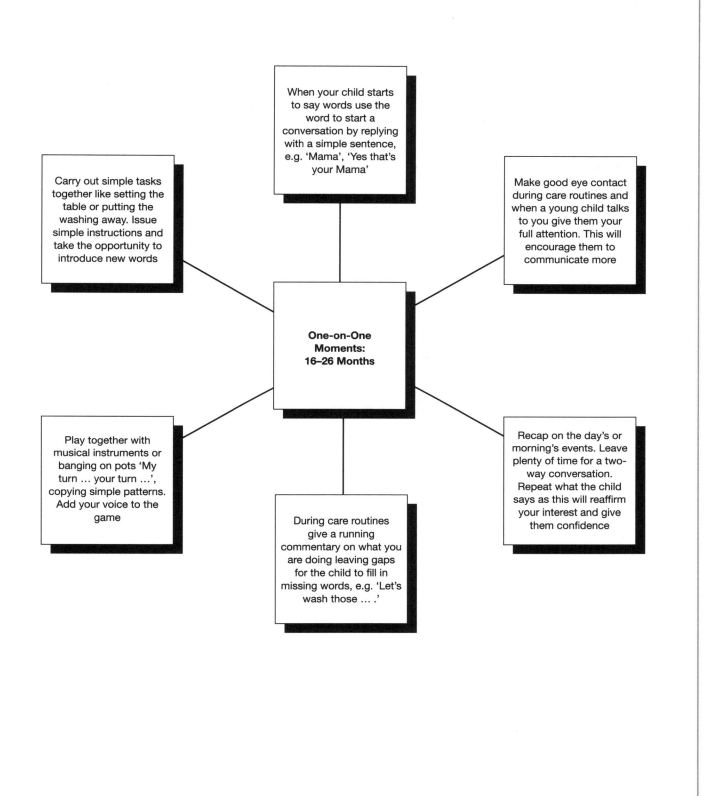

When your child starts to say words use the word to start a conversation by replying with a simple sentence, e.g. 'Mama', 'Yes that's your Mama'

Carry out simple tasks together like setting the table or putting the washing away. Issue simple instructions and take the opportunity to introduce new words

Make good eye contact during care routines and when a young child talks to you give them your full attention. This will encourage them to communicate more

One-on-One Moments: 16–26 Months

Play together with musical instruments or banging on pots 'My turn … your turn …', copying simple patterns. Add your voice to the game

During care routines give a running commentary on what you are doing leaving gaps for the child to fill in missing words, e.g. 'Let's wash those … .'

Recap on the day's or morning's events. Leave plenty of time for a two-way conversation. Repeat what the child says as this will reaffirm your interest and give them confidence

Developing Pre-School Communication and Language, Paul Chapman Publishing © Chris Dukes and Maggie Smith, 2007

Activities for a language-rich pre-school: 16–26 months

Physical development

We're going on a bear hunt

Read the Bear Hunt story (*We're Going on a Bear Hunt* by Michael Rosen) to the children. Be expressive with your voice and use exaggerated body movements to describe what the children in the story are doing. Take the children outside and suggest: 'Shall we go on a bear hunt?' Model the movements and encourage the children to join in the descriptions and the actions.

Knowledge and understanding of the world

Cleaning our garden

Toddlers love to be outdoors in any kind of weather. Regularly take the children outdoors with a variety of brushes and wastepaper bins. Show them how to help keep the garden clean and tidy. This might involve picking up leaves for use later during creative activities. Give the children a plant spray container and a cloth each to use to clean equipment such as bikes, scooters, etc. Encourage the children to wash the stairs, walls of the buildings, playhouse, etc. using the spray containers. Remember to stop half way for a reward of a snack break – have your impromptu picnic outside too. Describe to the children what you see them doing and encourage them to tell you what they are doing.

Personal, social and emotional development

Row the boat together

Using the song 'Row the Boat', pair children up and show them how to rock backwards and forwards while holding hands. Sing the song 'Row, row, row your boat gently up the stream' or have the song on a song tape. Not only is this great fun it encourages the children to interact and play cooperatively as well as listen to adult instructions.

Problem-solving, reasoning and numeracy

Whose shoes are these?

In small-group time, talk about shoes and encourage the children to show or talk about their own shoes, the colour, the fastenings, etc. Ask all of the children to take their shoes off. Place them in a pile in the middle of the floor. One at a time get the children to find their own shoes. Ask the children to 'help' each put their own shoes back on. Remember to look closely at the children's shoes before they take them off so you remember which shoes belong to which child. Put your own shoes into the pile and 'accidentally' take the wrong shoes out – wait for the children's delighted reactions!

Creative development

Natural collections in the water

Collect natural materials with the children such as sponges, shells, cork, stones, feathers, tree bark, etc. Some of this can be done either on a walk in the park or in the pre-school garden, some items can even be brought from home. Set children up with either individual basins or a shared water tray (transparent ones are the best). Allow the children to

explore the natural items in warm water. When they have finished, encourage the children to lay their 'collection' out to dry. The following day the same activity can be carried out in the sand. The opportunities to explore language and sounds are endless.

 Hands-on activity

Nowadays most pre-schools have a digital camera. Ask one of your friends to take a series of photographs of your face displaying different emotions such as smiling, looking sad, laughing, etc. Laminate the photographs so the children can handle them.

Show these photographs to your key group children when working one-to-one.

Get the children to copy your expressions and begin to teach them the language of emotions.

As an extension activity take photographs of the children copying your photographs. Show them back to the children. They can even be made into a 'Feelings Book'.

 Further reading

Meggitt, C. (2006) *Child Development: An Illustrated Guide*, 2nd edn. Heinemann.
Sheridan, M. D., Frost, M. and Shrama, A. (1997) *From Birth to Five Years: Children's Developmental Progress*, revised edn. Routledge.

CHAPTER FIVE

Toddlers and children: 22–36 months

In this chapter you will find:

▶ An overview of language development

▶ Appropriate expectations for children's development

▶ An outline of effective and reflective early years practice

▶ How to make the most of one-on-one moments

▶ Curriculum-based language-rich activities

▶ A hands-on activity

Overview 22–36 months

This is the age when young children are developing language and communication skills to keep pace with the contents of their own imagination. Progress with communication skills is rapid and those children who are struggling to express themselves and who may need support are beginning to become obvious to those who work closely with them. Sometimes these children will need only extra time and patience; others may require extra input and support from parents, practitioners and perhaps a speech and language therapist.

Lots of children of this age are already 'little conversationalists' who love to ask questions and can give simple replies. A sense of self is beginning to develop and most are not reticent at communicating with practitioners. Young children begin to express what they like or dislike and what they want and do not want to do. This is often called the 'terrible twos' but more likely any resulting behaviours are caused by the frustration of not being able to explain themselves clearly to those around them.

At this stage a child may have a range of 50–500 words or sounds. Those at the youngest developmental stage may just be beginning to be understood by those outside their immediate circle of family and friends. By the top end of this developmental stage those who are not so familiar with the child should be able to understand and make sense of what they are saying. There may still be mispronunciations and immature language quirks.

The relentless pace of language and communications development will be stimulated by the opportunities offered to children both at home and within the pre-school. The rich and well ordered environment offered by most pre-schools will go a long way to providing children with the stimulation and role models they need. Children should be encouraged to talk talk talk, as at this age practice really does make perfect. Practitioners become the audience for children and their active and friendly listening provides children with the validation and recognition they need to think of themselves as effective communicators.

Listening to children shows our respect for them and builds their self esteem.
(Petrie, 1997)

Understanding 22–36 Months: Appropriate Expectations

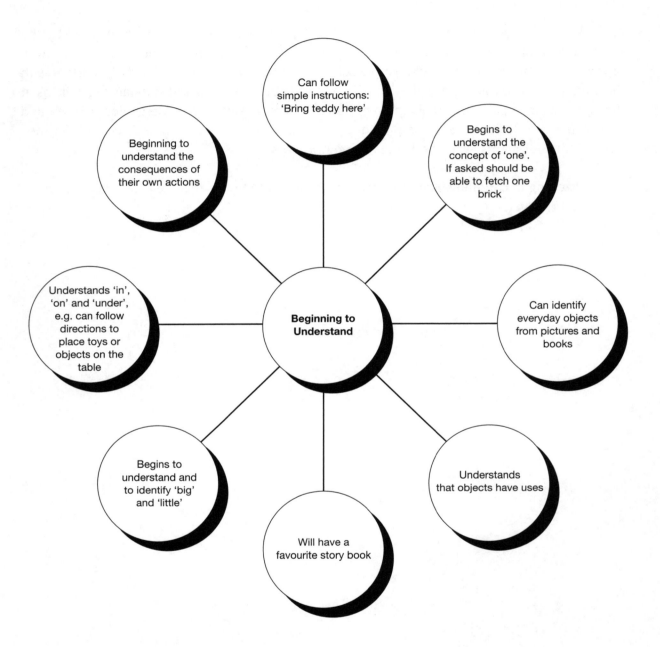

Can follow simple instructions: 'Bring teddy here'

Begins to understand the concept of 'one'. If asked should be able to fetch one brick

Beginning to understand the consequences of their own actions

Can identify everyday objects from pictures and books

Understands 'in', 'on' and 'under', e.g. can follow directions to place toys or objects on the table

Beginning to Understand

Understands that objects have uses

Begins to understand and to identify 'big' and 'little'

Will have a favourite story book

Remember, all children are different – some will exceed these expectations while others will be on their way to achieving them.

Developing Pre-School Communication and Language, Paul Chapman Publishing © Chris Dukes and Maggie Smith, 2007

Expressing 22–36 months: appropriate expectations

▶ Refers to him or herself by name

▶ Can combine 2–3 words to make a sentence, e.g. 'Me do it'

▶ Will initiate speaking to adults about everyday things

▶ Can repeat simple sentences

▶ Will comment to other children during play

▶ Uses negatives in phrases such as 'Not go' or 'No want'

▶ Joins in with some familiar songs and rhymes

▶ Uses 'my', 'mine', 'you' and 'me'

▶ Can answer simple Who, What or Where questions like 'What do we use to comb our hair?'

▶ Can take two or three turns in a conversation

▶ Asks lots of questions!

▶ Begins to talk about past events

▶ Starts to use the past tense such as 'stopped', 'pushed', but can over-generalise its use. e.g. 'drinked' instead of 'drank'

▶ Uses plurals, e.g. 'toys', 'babies'

What to look out for

▶ Withdrawn or quiet on a consistent basis

▶ Difficulty following simple instructions

▶ No interest in playing with others, even adults

▶ Unable to concentrate for more than a few seconds

▶ Uses only single or two-word phrases

▶ Frustration when trying to talk

▶ Speech which is difficult for familiar adults to understand

▶ Stammers (i.e. has periods of stammering that last longer than three months – this includes repeating sounds, parts of or whole words and not being able to get a sound started)

Effective Practice 22–36 Months

Ideas to introduce or consolidate

Talking is fun

Through the use of stories, songs, nursery rhymes and poems begin to have fun with language. Encourage children to join in and repeat key phrases and lines from books or songs, e.g. 'He huffed and he puffed' (*The Three Little Pigs*), 'What can you see?' (*Brown Bear*). Exaggerate words when telling stories such as 'sssssssssss snake' (support with hand actions), 'The giant went ooooooover the bridge' (make an arching movement with your arm). Use your body language and facial expressions and encourage the children to do the same thing.

Introduce children to nursery action songs such as 'The Wheels on the Bus', 'Incey Wincey Spider' etc. Invest in a good poetry book for use with children. Make sure you tell only very short poems with rhythm and rhyme. The children will not mind if they don't understand every word or the meaning as the fun will be in the telling or the reading and repeating. Children love the sound of limericks but often do not understand them. Remember, learning new words and extending vocabulary should be fun for both children and practitioner.

Learning and doing new things

Children learn new vocabulary from new experiences. Begin to prepare children for getting the most out of new experiences by encouraging *anticipation* and *prediction*.

For example, look at books and play with small world animals before a trip to the farm or zoo. If going swimming, set up an interactive display with the children of all the types of things you need to take when visiting a swimming pool.

'Think aloud' when around the children by asking them open questions such as 'I wonder what we will see at the zoo?' 'I wonder if the water will be warm at the swimming pool?'

Express your own ideas and thoughts such as 'I'm really looking forward to going on the bus to the zoo', 'I'm going to have a shower before I get into the swimming pool'.

Through actively preparing children for new experiences or even those everyday ones, practitioners can be sure they are helping children get the most out of the whole learning experience.

Helping and doing

Children of this age want to please the adults around them. Expand language comprehension skills by asking children to do small chores for you, e.g. '*Ask* Mary for the *pen*, please'. As children grow, their confidence, understanding and memory increase. Practitioners can begin to expand the numbers of key words in instructions, e.g. 'Go and *ask* Mary for the *red pen* please'.

Play instructional games with the children both indoor and outdoors such as simple stop-and-start games and marching games with instructions. Make them fun and not too serious and the children will enjoy looking and listening and doing. Those children who do not yet fully comprehend will be able to follow the lead of their peers.

Expand these activities to begin to introduce prepositions such as 'over', 'under', 'in' and 'out'. Consolidate these skills by demonstrating actions at story times with a teddy or doll and during table-top play with small world equipment and construction materials.

Listening and enjoying

By playing and talking with children in *small groups* or on a *one-to-one basis* practitioners encourage children to develop many skills.

Listening and attention skills are crucial in the development of good communication. Through talking and listening to children we show them that good communication is made up of two parts: being able to express yourself and listening to others.

Activities such as the sharing of books and story sacks, joining in simple games and actively playing together all provide opportunities for children to learn to listen to adults and their peers.

Children will begin to try out newly acquired vocabulary and other language skills. Practitioners should value these contributions and provide the time and space for children to experiment and try out. This provides a safe environment for the consolidation of skills children already have.

Please and thank you

Parents are usually the main instigators of good manners in young children but practitioners do have a crucial role to play. Through role modelling rather than insistence, practitioners show children that there are conventional rules in society. A cheery 'Good morning' and 'Thank you' by practitioners demonstrate to children the importance of such conventions. If some of the children in the group are bilingual practitioners should ask their parents to teach them how to say 'Hello' and 'Goodbye' as well as 'Thank you' in the child's home language.

Activities for a language-rich pre-school: 22–36 months

Physical development

Old-fashioned nursery rhyme dancing

Either indoors or outdoors get small groups of children to hold hands in a circle and introduce them to old-fashioned but favourite songs and circle games such as 'Ring o' Roses', 'Oats and Beans and Barley Grow', 'The Grand Old Duke of York', the 'Hokey Cokie' and 'The Farmer's in the Den', etc. Research the Internet or buy a book of circle nursery rhymes. At a team meeting draw up a list of all the circle games that staff are familiar with and share your knowledge with each other.

A good guide for organising these games is the younger the children, the smaller the group needs to be. Some children will need a lot of support to participate in these games but it is always worth the effort.

Knowledge and understanding of the world

Taste preparation and testing

Look at different fruits and vegetables with children, letting them hold and smell them. Get the children to help you peel and cut up the fruits and vegetables and arrange them in dishes. Ask

Making the Most of One-on-One Moments: 22–36 Months

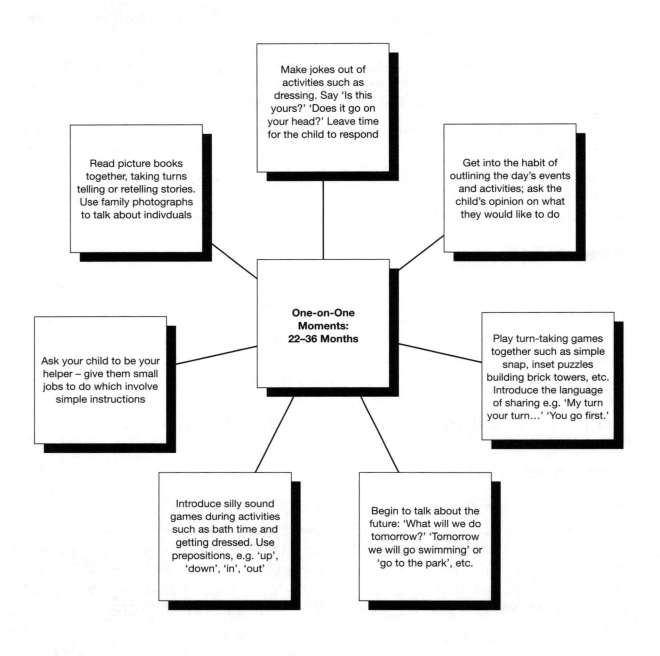

Make jokes out of activities such as dressing. Say 'Is this yours?' 'Does it go on your head?' Leave time for the child to respond

Read picture books together, taking turns telling or retelling stories. Use family photographs to talk about indivduals

Get into the habit of outlining the day's events and activities; ask the child's opinion on what they would like to do

One-on-One Moments: 22–36 Months

Ask your child to be your helper – give them small jobs to do which involve simple instructions

Play turn-taking games together such as simple snap, inset puzzles building brick towers, etc. Introduce the language of sharing e.g. 'My turn your turn…' 'You go first.'

Introduce silly sound games during activities such as bath time and getting dressed. Use prepositions, e.g. 'up', 'down', 'in', 'out'

Begin to talk about the future: 'What will we do tomorrow?' 'Tomorrow we will go swimming' or 'go to the park', etc.

Developing Pre-School Communication and Language, Paul Chapman Publishing © Chris Dukes and Maggie Smith, 2007

the children to close their eyes and taste-test small pieces, asking them to guess what they are eating. Ask them open questions, e.g. 'What does it taste/feel like?' etc.

Note: Check first if any of the children have any allergies to the foodstuffs being used. Also ask them before you start if there is anything they really don't like. Make sure that you avoid those items.

Personal, social and emotional development

A baby for you

Set up a display with lots of soft toys and dolls. At small-group time tell the children you are all going to sing 'Miss Polly had a Dolly who was sick ...' but that all of the children need to have a toy or dolly to hold. Explain that today instead of choosing your own dolly, everyone will get a chance to choose one for their friend. Send the children one at a time to choose a toy/doll and give it to a named child to hold for the duration of the song. This will help the children develop empathy, follow simple instructions as well as learn to give and accept from others.

Problem-solving, reasoning and numeracy

Guessing bag

Using a drawstring bag or a decorated pillow case, put a small selection of household objects inside. Ask children one at a time to put their hands into the bag and feel for an object. Ask the child to guess what the object is by feeling. Ask suitable open questions to encourage exploration of the object, e.g. 'Do you have one in your kitchen?' etc. After a short time let the child take the object out of the bag whether or not they have guessed what it is and give them positive praise for their efforts. With younger children it is often good to look at the objects together, naming them before putting them into the bag.

Creative development

Play dough bakery

Supply children with chef's hats, rolling pins, cookie cutters and baking trays, and a toy oven if available. Encourage the children to make suitable items for the baker's shop. Extend the play to include the setting up of a shop with paper bags, cash register with pennies, etc.

Remember some children will be happy to extend their play but some will be content to play their own game with the play dough. Facilitate the children's play only if they want you to.

Communication, language and literacy

Stories about us

Using a digital camera take photographs of the children in the pre-school at play and at other times of the day. During small-group time pin up one of the photographs and ask the children to tell you what was happening in the picture. Write what the children say underneath the picture and move on to the next one. The next day put the pictures in a scrap book with the children's words printed underneath. Show it to the children during story time and read back their words to them.

 Hands-on activity

Take the time in a busy week to carry out focused observations on your key work children to enable you to assess their language skills. These observations could be as long or as brief as you have time for. The aim is to give you a picture of the child's patterns of communication.

To remind yourself and colleagues to note down when you see a child talking either with another child or to a member of staff make a 'Chatterbox' badge for the child to wear – that way everyone can help you with your observations (see template below).

I'm a Chatterbox today

 Further reading

Meggitt, C. (2006) *Child Development: An Illustrated Guide*, 2nd edn. Heinemann.
Sheridan, M. D., Frost, M. and Shrama, A. (1997) *From Birth to Five Years: Children's Developmental Progress*, revised edn. Routledge.

CHAPTER SIX

Children: 30–50 months

In this chapter you will find:

▶ An overview of language development

▶ Appropriate expectations for children's development

▶ An outline of effective and reflective early years practice

▶ How to make the most of one-on-one moments

▶ Curriculum-based language-rich activities

▶ A hands-on activity

Overview: 30–50 months

Children of this age, once settled, are generally filled with eagerness to go to 'their' pre-school. (*Of course there are often exceptions and those children who may experience temporary upsets during their pre-school life.*)

Practitioners can expect youngsters to respond enthusiastically to simple instructions, avidly join in or perhaps watchfully listen to any singing/nursery rhyme sessions. Pre-school sessions with these children are generally lively and fun although practitioners may often find themselves sorting out misunderstandings and conflicts between children.

Making choices and making friends with their peers are just two of the many challenges these youngsters face. Learning to become a skilful communicator will support children to achieve these aims. Difficulties and misunderstandings can occur when children do not have the language skills needed to support the making and building of friendships and relationships with their peers. Teaching young children to listen to each other is one of the challenges practitioners face.

The language of decision-making and the language of friendship both need to be role modelled and informally taught to children of this age and stage. Involving children in the daily planning routines can also help them feel involved and asking children to be a 'helper' can help ensure they feel part of the pre-school community.

Most children will have the ability to express their own needs using short phrases or sentences. This may be replaced by or accompanied by expressive gestures. Practitioners would and should show concern if children of this developmental stage are not able to do this.

Throughout this stage of development children often move from watching and 'taking in' to wholeheartedly joining in and becoming a keen member of the pre-school community. Practitioners continue to observe children to plan how they can best support them through the many challenges and changes that occur.

Children's individual personalities and an often unique way of learning can now become apparent. Practitioners need to be flexible in their approach to help children reach their own potential. The rewards are great as children move from simple expression to listening and contributing to often complex discussions.

Understanding 30–50 Months: Appropriate Expectations

Understands sentences with up to six key words

Enjoys jokes and plays on words

Can anticipate and tell you what might happen next in a story book or programme

Understands and can remember details from a story

Beginning to Understand

Follow three-step instructions, e.g. 'Find your shoes, put on your coat and sit down.'

Understands words referring to concepts such as size, position and space

Is able to shift attention from what they are doing, listen to comment and go back to the activity

Understands most words for common actions, objects and descriptions

Remember, all children are different – some will exceed these expectations while others will be on their way to achieving them.

Developing Pre-School Communication and Language, Paul Chapman Publishing © Chris Dukes and Maggie Smith, 2007

Expressing 30–50 months: appropriate expectations

▶ Will seek out and enjoy playing with peers

▶ Uses imagination and make-believe in play, especially role play

▶ Can tell stories which refer to past events, in some detail and in the correct sequence

▶ May have a vocabulary of up to a thousand words

▶ Uses more complex sentences of four or more words

▶ Can hold a short conversation with a variety of people

▶ Uses most basic grammatical structures such as the past tense with only a few mistakes

▶ Can express their own ideas and feelings

▶ Ask lots of questions, especially 'How?' and 'Why?' questions.

▶ Speech is generally clear with a few immaturities

What to look out for

▶ Has difficulties or is not interested in playing with peers

▶ Has no interest in stories and shows little imagination

▶ Unable to follow simple instructions

▶ Unable to concentrate for more than a few minutes

▶ Has a small vocabulary and finds it hard to construct a sentence

▶ Unable to answer a simple question such as 'What is this?'

▶ Speech is difficult to understand even by familiar adults

▶ Stammers (i.e. has periods of stammering lasting longer than three months – this includes repeating sounds, parts of or whole words and not being able to get a sound started)

Effective Practice 30–50 Months

Ideas to introduce or consolidate

Joining in and helping

In order for children to vocalise and join in with the pre-school routines they need to be encouraged by practitioners to become part of the nursery community.

One of the main aims for practitioners is having the expectation that children will join in and enjoy doing things together. There are many different strategies that can be used to help children find their voice, e.g. when it is tidy-up time practitioners could say 'Let's all tidy up' then ask the children 'What are we going to do?' This strategy can be used throughout the day to ensure that children understand what to do as well as helping them feel part of the group. Those children who perhaps don't understand what is being asked of them should be encouraged to take their lead from their peers and copy what they are doing – a group visual timetable often helps all children to feel secure within the nursery routines.

When children are 'helping' with nursery chores practitioners are able to initiate a conversation through the use of open-ended questions and through making their own personal statements, e.g. 'Let's cut up the fruit together', 'I love apples they taste good', 'What do you think of apples?' In this case the practitioner has left the door open for the child to say as little or as much as he or she wants while providing an opportunity to mimic their own language.

'Who does this belong to?'

Show-and-tell experiences, interactive displays and everyday routines such as putting coats on provide practitioners with the opportunity to extend the use of pronouns within the setting. By introducing and modelling the use of words such as 'me', 'yours', 'mine', 'you', etc. the practitioner is providing children with rich language experiences. 'Forgetting' which child owns a particular coat or toy provides practitioners with the opportunity to get children using personal pronouns such as 'It's mine' or 'I brought that'.

Time to talk

Practitioners can give children the opportunity to practise and learn new skills by asking them to respond to and recall recent experiences as well as predicting what new experiences will be like.

By giving young children the time and space to talk about the many things that happen at home and at the weekend practitioners provide a real opportunity for children to develop useful skills such as talking and listening as well as building confidence.

Children love the familiarity of retold stories and often volunteer to tell the middle or ending of a well-loved tale. Story packs provide visual clues and props which encourage children to develop their retelling skills.

Children can be encouraged to recall events such as parties, concerts or trips. Practitioners can also promote prediction skills by asking them to anticipate what might happen on future occasions.

Talking together

Children need to further develop their conversational skills and explore language in a deeper, more meaningful way. This can be provided through opportunities to explore and develop language around a single subject. These conversations do not have to be long or forced but once initiated will develop in a natural way.

> An example of extending a conversation with a child is:
>
> 'I like your hat.'
>
> 'Did you go with Mummy to buy it?'
>
> '*Why* did you choose this one?'
>
> '*Did* they have other hats you liked in the shop?'
>
> '*What* were they like?'
>
> 'I would like to get a hat like this for my little boy.'
>
> This may seem contrived but is an essential tool for extending children's conversational skills.

Talking and listening

Practitioners will be able to extend listening and attention skills by the use of short interactive 'carpet times'. Children love to talk and listen but attention spans differ widely. By providing children with short active bursts of group time/carpet time, practitioners are providing the opportunity both to talk and listen together. Visual props such as story sacks encourage children's engagement and participation. Those children with short attention skills should be accommodated in smaller groups for shorter amounts of time.

A rule of thumb is that children can be expected to concentrate only the same number of minutes as their age plus 5, e.g. a three-year-old should sit for only 3 minutes plus 5 minutes giving a total of 8 minutes **maximum** concentration time.

Sharing a joke

Children of this age love to laugh and joke. Funny stories can often cause great hilarity within any pre-school. Encourage children's listening skills by occasionally making mistakes that they can correct, e.g. 'There goes that little dog again' (when it's a cat). Children will tune in to hear if they can pick up any other 'mistakes'.

Use story books such as *How Do I Put It On?* (Shigeo Watanabe) to share a joke with a small group of children. By using visual props or books practitioners are ensuring that *all* children will be in on the joke or funny story.

Now and then

Many pre-school activities provide practitioners with the opportunity to introduce the idea of time to children. By introducing the days of the week, the mornings and the afternoons, school days and the weekend practitioners are supporting children to make sense of their world and develop important communication skills. Children learn to modify their spoken language accordingly, e.g. 'After pre-school Mum and I are going to the park', 'At Christmas we are going to my Nan's' etc.

The language of some songs and rhymes, visual timetables and daily registration as well as festivals and special days such as birthdays, ensure that children are introduced to these ideas. Through role modelling speech types and tenses practitioners can ensure that they are supporting children to understand these difficult concepts.

I learnt most not from those who taught me, but from those who talked with me. *(St Augustine)*

Making the Most of One-on-One Moments: 30–50 Months

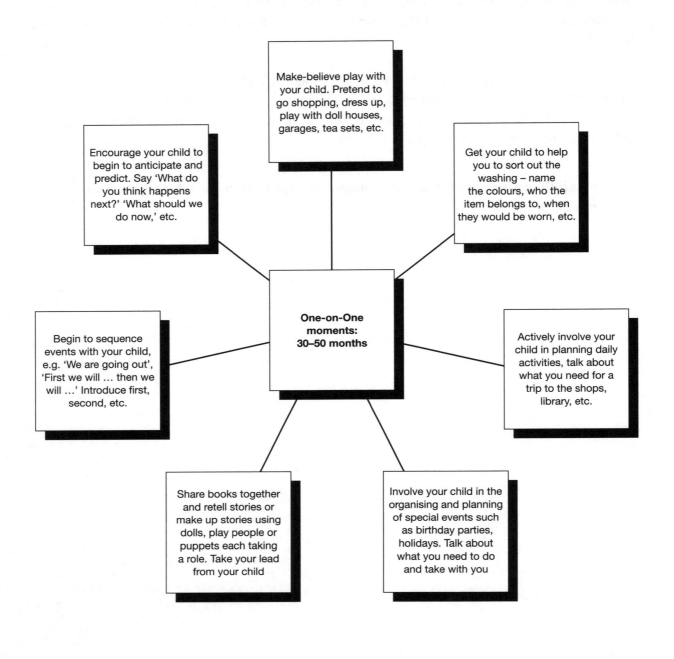

Make-believe play with your child. Pretend to go shopping, dress up, play with doll houses, garages, tea sets, etc.

Encourage your child to begin to anticipate and predict. Say 'What do you think happens next?' 'What should we do now,' etc.

Get your child to help you to sort out the washing – name the colours, who the item belongs to, when they would be worn, etc.

Begin to sequence events with your child, e.g. 'We are going out', 'First we will … then we will …' Introduce first, second, etc.

One-on-One moments: 30–50 months

Actively involve your child in planning daily activities, talk about what you need for a trip to the shops, library, etc.

Share books together and retell stories or make up stories using dolls, play people or puppets each taking a role. Take your lead from your child

Involve your child in the organising and planning of special events such as birthday parties, holidays. Talk about what you need to do and take with you

Activities for a language-rich pre-school: 30–50 months

Physical development

Windy day kites

On a windy day give the children pre-cut kite shapes made from thin card or sugar paper. Encourage the children to attach paper streamers or ribbons. Attach a piece of string making a hoop for the child to put their hand through. Run with children on a clear playground (put all other toys away first) or in the park or a field. Children will love the sensation of trailing the kite behind them. Encourage the children to sing or shout as they run helping them find their 'loud voice'.

Note: Kites made with paper or card will not last – it is the running and fun that is important rather than the end product.

Knowledge and understanding of the world

Road safety skills

This is a good time to introduce the idea of road safety to children. Invite a community police-man/woman to your setting or your local lollipop person to talk to the children. Introduce books and photographs about developing road sense to the children at story time. Set up a road track in the pre-school garden which has directional arrows for children to follow on wheeled toys. Make a large zebra crossing indoors with the children using black and white sugar paper. Place this outside on the track and encourage the children to practise crossing while the children in the wheeled toys stop for the pedestrians. Reinforce the spoken words with road signs and the printed word.

Note: Remember to involve parents in these activities as much as possible and inform them that you are discussing road safety with their child. This is very important as parents will want to reinforce their child's learning.

Personal social and emotional development

Camping out

In key worker groups or in small groups sit down with the children and talk about camping out and making tents, a good started point is *Camping Out* in the Usborne Farmyard Tales series by Heather Amery and Stephen Cartwright. Show the children your equipment – a blanket, pillows, a sheet, a torch, etc. – and together plan your adventure. The adult role is to facilitate and help the children turn their ideas into reality. Encourage the children to work cooperatively in the making of the camp. Once the tent is set up and the play and talk is flowing the adult should withdraw. As a special treat allow the children to have their snack in their tent.

Problem-solving, reasoning and numeracy

What can I be?

Again in pairs play riddle games and guessing games with children. Ask the children to listen closely and guess what you are. Initially give your clues to objects and people in categories, e.g. animals, vehicles, people who help us, etc. Once children get good at the game you can mix and match the things you choose. For an elephant you could say, 'I am very large; I have a long trunk; I live in Africa. What am I?' For a fire engine, you could say, 'I am big and red; I have a long ladder and four wheels; I have a loud siren; I help put out fires. What am I?'

It is helpful to have a representation of the object or person to show afterwards, or if they find the riddle too difficult, photographs and books could also be used.

Creative development

Making spells

Using clean compost give the children some compost in a dish or bucket to mix with water (this activity by itself could hold the child's attention for some time). Encourage the children to go into the garden and look for things to put into their 'magic bucket' or you could supply children with a variety of collage materials such as wood chippings, crushed leaves, petals, etc. Help children to make up spells like Meg and Mog in the books by Helen Nicoll and Jan Pienkowski (Puffin Paperbacks). Put the 'spells' somewhere safe overnight so the children can return to them the next day. Talk to the children about their magic bucket and its contents etc.

Communication, language and literacy

Rhythm shakers

Make small shakers with children by placing dried beans or peas inside empty yoghurt pots. Remember to check they are well sealed. Alternatively buy small hand-held shakers such as the ones commercially available shaped liked eggs. Allow children to shake and use them listening to music and dancing. Once the novelty of the shaker has worn off, use it for a structured listening activity.

During small-group time or key-worker time get the children to copy simple patterns of beats and shakes. It is a good idea to start the activity 'shaking' each child's name in the circle. The adult demonstrates and the children copy. As the activity becomes more successful increase the number of beats children have to listen to and copy. Some children will require a lot of support to participate in this activity. Keep the activity short and fun.

 Hands-on activity

Get into the habit of providing children with books alongside small world and imaginative play activities. They may use the books to develop their play and language skills but accept that they may not be interested in them sometimes if absorbed in a play experience.

In a staff meeting draw up a list of suitable books to use. Here are one or two to get you started:

▶ Block play or with construction materials: *The Three Little Pigs*

▶ Farm animals: *Mr Gumpy's Outing*, by John Burningham

 Further reading

Amery, H. (2005) *Camping Out*, illust. Stephen Cartwright, new edn, Mini Farmyard Tales Series. Usbourne Publishing.

Burningham, J. (2001) *Mr Grumpy's Outing*, new edn. RedFox.

Lewis, J. (illust.) (1999) *Three Little Pigs*, First Favourite Tales Series. Ladybird Books.

Meggitt, C. (2006) Child Development: An Illustrated Guide, 2nd edn. Heinemann.

Nicoll, H. and Pienkowski, J. (1975) *Meg and Mog*, new edn. Picture Puffin.

Sheridan, M. D., Frost, M. and Sharma, A. (1997) *From Birth to Five Years: Children's Developmental Progress*, revised edn. Routledge.

Watanabe, S. (1993) *How Do I Put It On?*, illust. Yasuo Ohtomo, Red Fox Picture Books Series, Red Fox.

CHAPTER SEVEN

Children: 40–60 months

In this chapter you will find:

▶ An overview of language development

▶ Appropriate expectations for children's development

▶ An outline of effective and reflective early years practice

▶ How to make the most of one-on-one moments

▶ Curriculum-based language-rich activities

▶ A hands-on activity

Overview: 40–60 months

Children in this developmental group are generally the top end of any pre-school. These children typically are keen to please the adults around them. Generally they respond well to praise and are always ready to have fun. They are beginning to listen well and have a large bank of words they can draw upon to express themselves and even negotiate with practitioners and parents.

The spoken word can be used to gain the attention of the children and adults around them. The influence of older siblings and outside elements such as television can lead to language experimentation and may involve the use of words that practitioners would rather not hear in the pre-school! Practitioners need to show patience and recognise that exploration of language at this stage of development may often involve trial and error. Feeling comfortable and settled in their environment allows children the opportunity to begin to build up their growing vocabulary and confidence as effective communicators.

Although a child's communication and language are rapidly increasing practitioners sometimes presume these, still very young, children understand more than they actually do. This can often lead to misunderstandings and the appearance of non-compliance. Adults need to 'check out' verbally that children actually know what is expected of them.

This is a time of intense discovery and children at this developmental stage need to be provided with opportunities to explore, discover, create and experiment through their own 'hands-on' experiences.

The range of language will be broad, with some children anticipating, describing, retelling and speaking clearly. Others may even have moved into the new and exciting discovery of pre-reading skills with sounds, letters and words, while others may be struggling with specific sounds, have underdeveloped attention skills or struggle with comprehension. The challenge for practitioners is to understand individual learning needs and to meet those needs. In some cases this may mean working closely with other professionals such as speech and language therapists, in all cases working closely with the child's parents.

Reading and writing float on a sea of talk. *(James Britton, educationalist)*

Understanding 40–60 Months: Appropriate Expectations

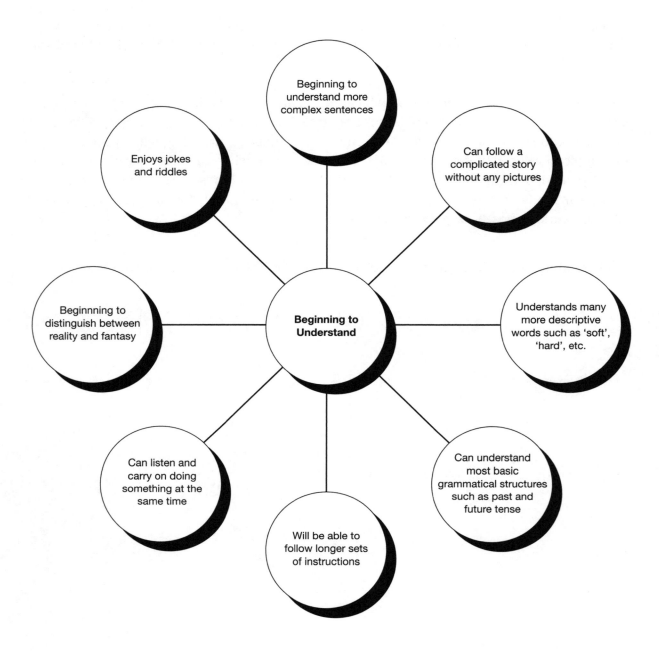

- Beginning to understand more complex sentences
- Can follow a complicated story without any pictures
- Understands many more descriptive words such as 'soft', 'hard', etc.
- Can understand most basic grammatical structures such as past and future tense
- Will be able to follow longer sets of instructions
- Can listen and carry on doing something at the same time
- Beginnning to distinguish between reality and fantasy
- Enjoys jokes and riddles

Beginning to Understand

Remember, all children are different – some will exceed these expectations while others will be on their way to achieving them

 Developing Pre-School Communication and Language, Paul Chapman Publishing © Chris Dukes and Maggie Smith, 2007

Expressing 40–60 months: appropriate expectations

▶ Can express themselves well with a vocabulary of thousands of words

▶ Recounts a story accurately with details and in the correct sequence

▶ Starts to make predictions about what will happen next in a story book or TV programme

▶ Can explain what words mean and what things are used for

▶ Can answer 'How?' and 'Why?' questions

▶ Starts to ask 'When?' questions

▶ Can answer hypothetical questions like 'What would you do if …?' and give a reason for the answer

▶ Can have a conversation with a variety of people about a range of topics

▶ Cooperates with peers in activities and play

▶ Uses imagination and make-believe to act out and role play

▶ Speech is generally clear

▶ Continues to speak with a few grammatical errors, e.g. 'drinked'

What to look out for

▶ Unable to hold or understand a conversation

▶ Does not use complete sentences

▶ Difficulty in following routines or instructions

▶ Does not want to interact with peers or adults

▶ Poor attention and concentration

▶ Stammering

▶ Unclear speech

Note: All speech sounds should be correct by the age of 6–7 years.

Effective Practice 40–60 Months

Ideas to introduce or consolidate

Giving and accepting a point of view

Throughout their lives children have been listening and watching those around them. They are now beginning to understand their world and, more importantly, their place in that world.

They have learned how to communicate with others from watching their parents, brothers and sisters and from the practitioners who look after them.

Young children are beginning to understand that to get others to listen to their needs, wants and point of view *they* also need to learn to listen. Through role modelling attentive listening skills practitioners show children that they are worth listening to and that their point of view is valid.

In calm relaxed pre-school settings where everyone can talk and get a fair hearing young children begin to learn to take their place in the wider community. Children can learn to identify with and begin to understand their peers and their immediate circle of family and friends. Story time, circle time and one-on-one moments all help teach children the worthwhile skills and language of sympathy and compassion. Turn-taking and listening games support children develop the other skills they need in order to participate in conversation and begin to develop their own viewpoint.

Practitioners should recognise that they are giving children life skills when they teach them to be good communicators. Towards the end of a child's pre-school life these skills will be crucial in ensuring positive transitions onto other settings or school.

Yesterday, today and tomorrow

Children of this age need to begin to understand that actions and events occur in an order. Practitioners should offer children sequencing activities, routines and even visual timetables to help promote this concept.

The idea of time is a hard one for children to understand. Research shows that children understand the past tense earlier than the future tense.

By keeping a daily record practitioners can talk to the children about what they did yesterday before recapping on what happened today and planning what will happen tomorrow.

During daily activities practitioners should begin to talk about what a child is doing, what he or she has done and what he or she is going to do in an everyday context. Practitioners should talk to the children about what they are doing, e.g. 'Are you going to ride the bike?' 'Look, you're riding the bike' and afterwards 'I watched you ride the bike earlier on today'.

Stories that involve time reinforce the concept, e.g. story of the *Three Little Pigs* – what they planned, what they did and what happened afterwards.

Practitioners should be aware that this is a difficult concept for children to understand. Some children may be interested and appear to understand while others might find the concepts confusing. Take your lead from the children and if you think they are ready introduce these ideas in a real and everyday natural way.

Listening and doing

We all live in a world where we need to listen to instructions and follow them. There are times such as during a fire drill where listening and doing are not optional. Creating a pre-school community where children listen to adults and each other is a prerequisite for a successful setting. Regular routines, specific listening activities such as dance, movement, playing musical instruments, sound lotto games, etc. all support practitioners to help children develop good listening skills.

At this developmental stage practitioners can move children on from passive listening by ensuring that they do participate to the best of their ability, cooperate when asked to do so, and follow instructions when needed.

Note: It is always a good idea to praise the children who are listening and following instructions rather than drawing attention to those who are not. Saying 'We will' rather than 'You will' builds upon the idea of a pre-school community working together. Similarly, by mentioning individual children by name when issuing a general instruction usually ensures cooperation.

'I know lots of words'

Children of this age need to be able to expand their vocabulary, i.e. they need to have a large bank of words to draw upon and use.

Everyday life and the whole pre-school experience are rich with words.

Practitioners need to help children to sort the words they know as well as learn new words. All types of nursery activities lend themselves to this. Snack time provides the perfect opportunity for children to increase their vocabulary with regard to fruit and food. When children are younger all fruit may have been a 'nana' (banana) but as a child grows older they begin to realise that there are in fact lots of types of fruits. Practitioners should help children expand their vocabulary and begin to categorise the words they need. This can be done by naming everyday fruits and having planned activities such as tasting sessions to introduce new words for taste and texture as well as colours.

The aim for the practitioner is to understand what children already know (through observation) and work out ways to help them expand their vocabulary. This can be done by using the whole range of the curriculum.

Making the Most of One-on-One Moments: 40–60 Months

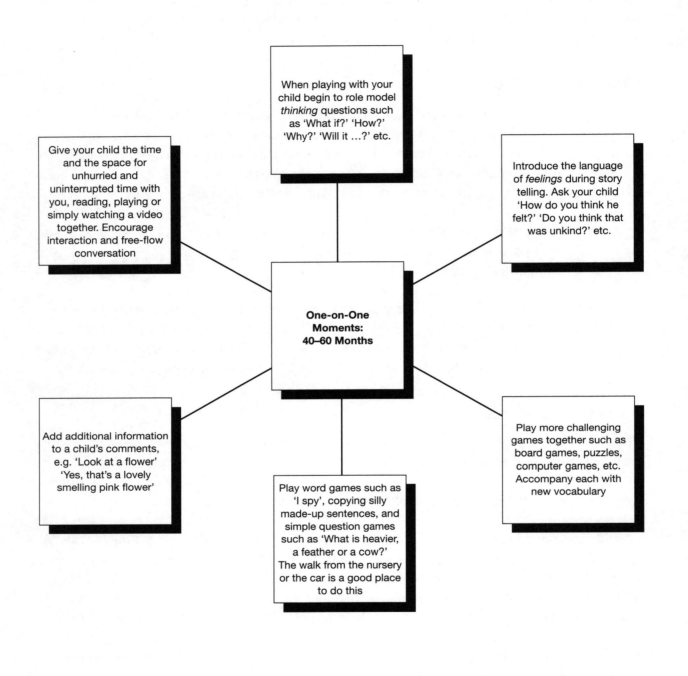

When playing with your child begin to role model *thinking* questions such as 'What if?' 'How?' 'Why?' 'Will it …?' etc.

Give your child the time and the space for unhurried and uninterrupted time with you, reading, playing or simply watching a video together. Encourage interaction and free-flow conversation

Introduce the language of *feelings* during story telling. Ask your child 'How do you think he felt?' 'Do you think that was unkind?' etc.

One-on-One Moments: 40–60 Months

Add additional information to a child's comments, e.g. 'Look at a flower' 'Yes, that's a lovely smelling pink flower'

Play word games such as 'I spy', copying silly made-up sentences, and simple question games such as 'What is heavier, a feather or a cow?' The walk from the nursery or the car is a good place to do this

Play more challenging games together such as board games, puzzles, computer games, etc. Accompany each with new vocabulary

Developing Pre-School Communication and Language, Paul Chapman Publishing © Chris Dukes and Maggie Smith, 2007

Activities for a language-rich pre-school: 40–60 months

Physical development

Pirates and crocodiles

This game can be played either indoors or outdoors, using place mats, blocks, planks, tunnels and anything else that children can stand on or get into around a large space. Ask the children to run, skip, or jump around the space between the objects. When they hear you call out 'A crocodile is approaching' they must get themselves onto a safe place where their feet are not touching the ground. When you shout 'It's safe' they should resume their moving around. This is a very exciting game that helps develop good listening skills as well as being a lot of fun.

Knowledge and understanding of the world

Washing day

Choose a windy morning to help the children to set up a washing line outdoors. Wonder aloud where the best place might be to do this and follow the children's advice. Ask the children to collect some clothes from dolls and the home corner. Set the children up with basins of soapy water and get them to wash the clothes, cloths and anything else they bring. Show the children how to squeeze out the materials and hang them outside on the washing line. Throughout the day check the clothes to see which ones are drying first. Later in the day during a small circle time have a discussion about the drying properties of the wind and the sun. Get the children to predict what might have happened if the rain had come on etc.

Personal social and emotional development

Learning to be friends

Small circle time or group time can be used effectively to help children understand how our words and actions affect others. Using a persona doll/puppet or teddy and a ball, tell the children the story about how .... has got no one to play with her and her new ball. Say that .... admits that in the past she has called some of the other children names and has not always been very good at sharing her toys. Discuss this scenario from both ....'s point of view and the point of view of the other children. Finally ask the children how .... can win her friends back. Do not rush this activity and take your lead from the children. Try to make sure every child who wants to contribute can and remember the three-second rule (allow children up to three seconds to reply). At the end of the activity recap the things the children have said to the group.

Problem-solving, reasoning and numeracy

'Who am I thinking of?'

Before story time or during any quiet break say to the children 'I'm thinking about one of you. The person I am thinking about has…' then go on to slowly describe the child by identifying their clothes, the colour of their hair, the things they like, etc. The children will soon catch on and will begin scanning the group trying to match your descriptions to what they see. Try to catch the children out sometimes by describing another member of staff (if present) or yourself.

Creative development

Magic flour drawing

Lightly cover a surface with flour or get the children to sieve flour onto a surface. Show the children how to draw or write into the flour with their fingers. When they want a new surface get them to lightly sieve flour over their drawing. Once the activity is over get the children to use a dustpan and brush to sweep away the remaining flour. The flour could be used later for a mixing activity. Take every opportunity to introduce new vocabulary and listen to the children's descriptions of what they are doing.

Communication, language and literacy

The beep game

Explain to the children that during the telling of a well loved story, song or nursery rhyme you are going to get some of the words wrong. If they hear a wrong word they must shout 'bleep'. Demonstrate the activity with another team member so the children get the idea. The children will listen intently to pick up on your 'mistakes'.

 Hands-on activity

During weekly planning meetings agree on a set of key words that all practitioners will try to use during the following week. Make the words relevant to the week's activities.

Write the words in large letters and place them around the room to remind practitioners (the children will be interested in them as well).

Write them on your parents' notice board or hand out a list for parents to reinforce at home.

Ask parents if they have words they would like to add to your list.

Build up a folder of key words for different activities.

 Further reading

Meggitt, C. (2006) *Child Development: An Illustrated Guide*, 2nd edn. Heinemann.

Sheridan, M. D., Frost, M. and Sharma, A. (1997) *From Birth to Five Years: Children's Developmental Progress*, revised edn. Routledge.

CHAPTER EIGHT
Working with young bilingual learners

In this chapter we aim to provide practitioners with a greater understanding of how young bilingual children learn additional languages, and to provide practitioners with tried and tested strategies to support the language development of these children.

You will find:

▶ An overview of working with young bilingual learners

▶ Ideas on how to create a supportive environment for bilingual children

▶ Some basic facts and terms used

▶ The Golden Rules of working with young bilingual children

▶ A range of strategies to use when working with young bilingual children

▶ A hands-on activity

Overview

While most children and adults in Britain are monolingual, that is speak only one language and that one mainly English, this is not the case in many parts of the world. Being bilingual or learning a second language should in no way be viewed as a difficulty. In fact, research suggests that bilingualism can benefit children's overall academic and intellectual development and progress. It also shows that consistent and adequate input in both languages produces the best results.

Language is important for many social and cultural reasons. A child's sense of personal and cultural identity is supported through their use of language. Practitioners therefore need to ensure that languages and cultures other than English are celebrated and valued within the pre-school.

The need to communicate with the parents, grandparents, extended family and friends of children is paramount for practitioners. These groups may use a variety of different languages. Some children may be in the position of perhaps one day returning to their place of origin or may throughout their schooling take extended holidays abroad. Every child's situation will be different, as will their needs; however, the quality of their experience will depend on the quality of the relationship and interaction with significant adults and peers in both languages.

Practitioners should be aware that by creating language-rich environments and using those strategies outlined below which are primarily aimed at supporting children who are learning English as a second or additional language, they will be supporting the language development of all of their pre-school children as all of the strategies discussed in this chapter are good for *all* children.

Creating a Supportive Environment for Bilingual Learners

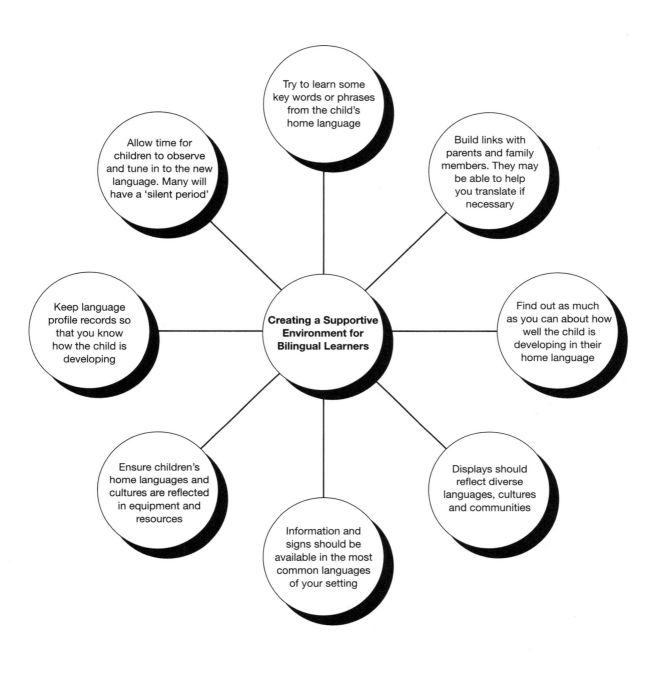

Try to learn some key words or phrases from the child's home language

Allow time for children to observe and tune in to the new language. Many will have a 'silent period'

Build links with parents and family members. They may be able to help you translate if necessary

Keep language profile records so that you know how the child is developing

Creating a Supportive Environment for Bilingual Learners

Find out as much as you can about how well the child is developing in their home language

Ensure children's home languages and cultures are reflected in equipment and resources

Information and signs should be available in the most common languages of your setting

Displays should reflect diverse languages, cultures and communities

Developing Pre-School Communication and Language, Paul Chapman Publishing © Chris Dukes and Maggie Smith, 2007

Basic facts and terms

▶ A child's 'first language' is any language learned before the age of three.

▶ A language learned after the age of three is considered to be a 'second' or 'additional' language.

▶ English is the recognised language in Britain and is therefore often referred to as the 'majority' language.

▶ Any other language spoken at home is therefore referred to as the 'minority' or 'heritage' language.

▶ If a child learns one language up to the age of three and then learns a 'second' or 'additional' language, the learning process is referred to as 'sequential bilingualism', i.e. one language is learned after another. In this case a child will have a grasp of the basic rules of the first language; and the better developed the first language, the easier it will be to learn the second language.

▶ If a child learns two (or more) languages from birth, this is referred to as 'simultaneous bilingualism', i.e. both languages are learned at the same time. It has been found that where one parent or family member speaks only one language and the other parent or another family member speaks only the other, children find it easier to separate and learn the two languages.

What it feels like to be a young bilingual learner arriving at pre-school

Imagine what it might be like to suddenly find yourself in an environment where you are not able to understand what anyone says and they are not able to understand you. If you can do this, you will already be able to be able to guess how a child, who speaks little or no English, might feel on starting at your pre-school.

Feelings of overwhelming strangeness, confusion, frustration and isolation are common. So too, however, is the desire to communicate which will be the motivation for learning a new language.

 Hands-on activity

Ask any bilingual parents you know to read several of your favourite picture books in their own language. Make a tape of the stories and use them sometimes at story time.

It is a good idea to ask them to speak slightly slower and record a sound such as a short ring of a bell when it is time to turn the page.

Some common patterns

▶ A child may have a 'silent' period.

▶ It is common for children to say little or nothing for up to seven months.

▶ Some children may show a reluctance to participate. This may be because toys or activities are unfamiliar, a lack of confidence or simply because the child needs time to watch and observe others.

▶ You may hear some code mixing – this means that children may mix and use words from two languages in one sentence. It is common in children who are in the early stages of learning two languages simultaneously and will continue until they are able to separate the two sets of vocabulary.

▶ You may hear imitation of whole phrases or sentences. A child may copy phrases and sentences in order to help them to join in with games and interact with their peers even if they are not sure exactly what is going on! This is often accompanied by actions and gestures which are also copied.

▶ You may observe rule mixing – this means that the child may mix and use the grammar and rules of the two languages. It can make their sentences sound very confused – by saying the words of a sentence in a strange order for example. This is part of the normal pattern of development and will continue until the child can separate the two language systems.

Remember:

Each child will have an individual pattern of progress and many things can affect language acquisition. These include motivation, self-confidence, anxiety levels, self-image, family circumstances and personality.

The Golden Rules

When Working with Young Bilingual Children

1. Remember young bilingual children may have a silent period. Give them time to try out and tune in.

2. Ensure all stories, songs and rhymes have clear illustrations and repeated actions and words.

3. Visual props should always be used.

4. Key words and phrases should always be repeated by the practitioner during activities.

5. Reflect the child's home language within your setting – ask parents for help to do this.

6. Value a child's home language – learn a few phrases.

7. Observe a child's spoken and non-spoken language. Keep records to show progress or difficulties.

8. Ask parents how a child's communication is in their home language. Do they comprehend and speak?

9. Use Makaton or non-verbal gestures to support your speech.

10. Model good use of English using clear natural speech. (Do not talk extra loudly!).

11. Use consistent routines so children know what is happening.

12. Use a whole-group visual timetable.

13. Give the child jobs that require no or little spoken language, e.g. handing out snacks and drinks.

14. Use the three-second rule, ask and wait.

15. Pair the silent child with a confident and fluent speaker during activities.

16. Praise often.

17. Accept minimal efforts to join in or communicate.

18. Make sure the child is placed third or fourth in turn-taking activities.

19. Carry out a home visit.

20. Be patient !

 Developing Pre-School Communication and Language, Paul Chapman Publishing © Chris Dukes and Maggie Smith, 2007

Strategies to Support Bilingual Learners

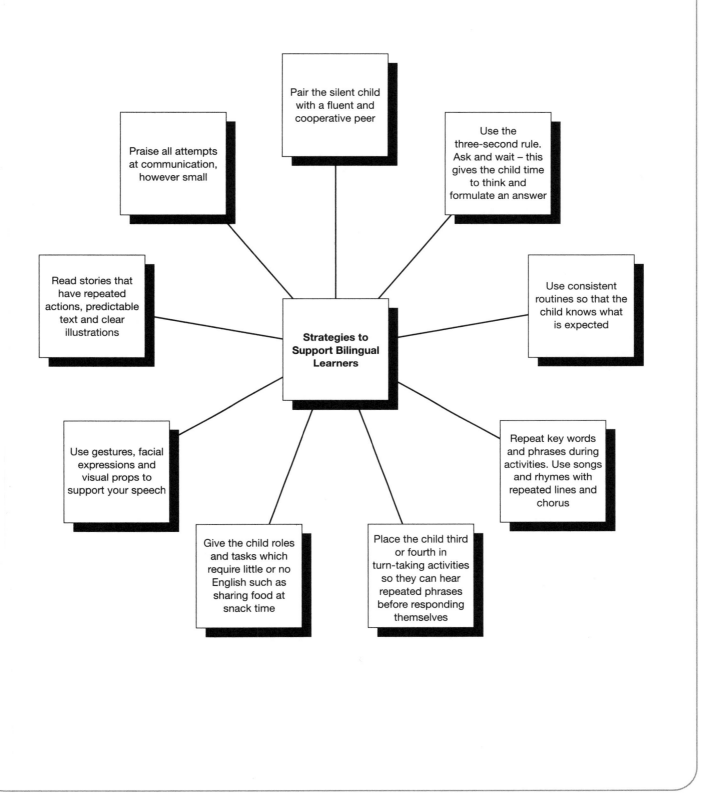

Pair the silent child with a fluent and cooperative peer

Praise all attempts at communication, however small

Use the three-second rule. Ask and wait – this gives the child time to think and formulate an answer

Read stories that have repeated actions, predictable text and clear illustrations

Strategies to Support Bilingual Learners

Use consistent routines so that the child knows what is expected

Use gestures, facial expressions and visual props to support your speech

Repeat key words and phrases during activities. Use songs and rhymes with repeated lines and chorus

Give the child roles and tasks which require little or no English such as sharing food at snack time

Place the child third or fourth in turn-taking activities so they can hear repeated phrases before responding themselves

Developing Pre-School Communication and Language, Paul Chapman Publishing © Chris Dukes and Maggie Smith, 2007

Further reading

Thompson, L. (1999) *Young Bilingual Learners in Nursery Schools*. Multilingual Matters.

CHAPTER NINE

Creating language opportunities in the pre-school

In this chapter we aim to show practitioners how language opportunities can be created in the pre-school by outlining:

▶ How to develop heuristic play with younger babies and children

▶ How to make a treasure basket

▶ How to use puppets and persona dolls

▶ How to make and use story sacks

▶ How to use circle time

▶ Examples of circle time activities

Heuristic play

Heuristic play with objects is a safe way for young children to satisfy their need for exploratory play, while offering an opportunity for practitioners to introduce new words to match the often sensory experiences.

The word 'heuristic' comes from the Greek language and translates as 'serves to discover'.

The adult role is mainly to provide babies and toddlers with the materials with which to explore. These items are usually presented in a traditional wicker basket. Opportunities for developing language and communication arise especially:

▶ when *introducing* the activity;

▶ from time to time *during* the activity (parts of this activity will be the child exploring the objects by themselves);

▶ again during the *tidying away* of the basket when the objects are being placed inside it ready to be put away.

Heuristic play offers practitioners a unique time when they can explore new language possibilities for even the youngest of babies.

During heuristic play children explore the objects provided for them on a rug on the floor. The objects are everyday ones and are usually presented to the child in a wicker basket. (See the diagram below for further suggestions and ideas about treasure baskets.)

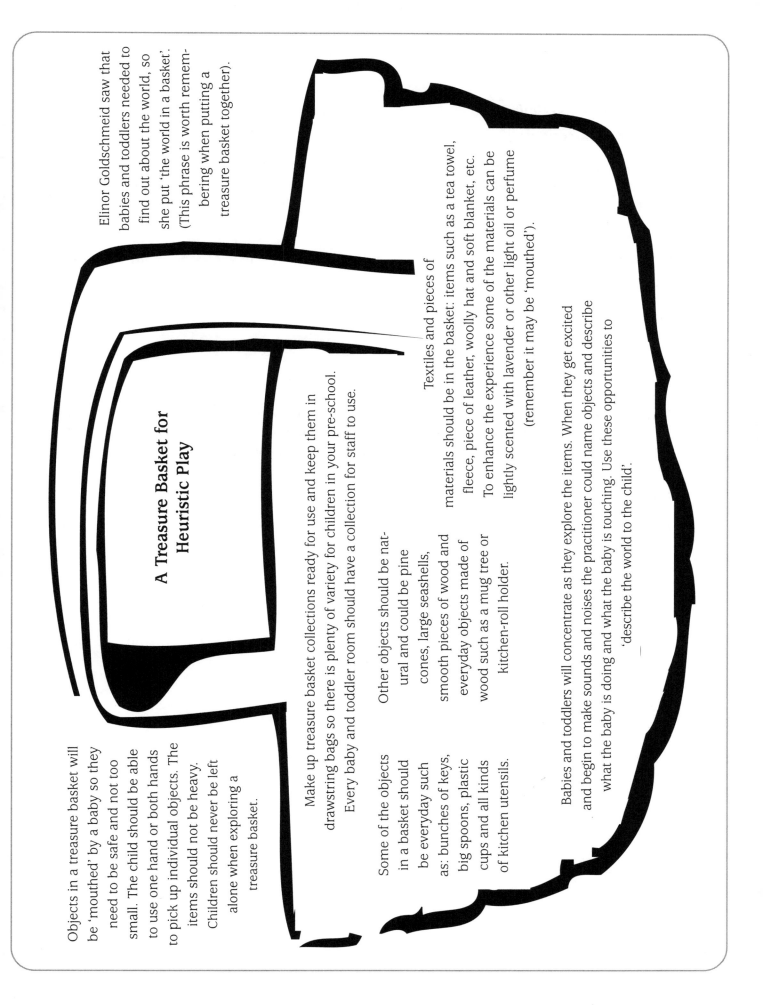

A Treasure Basket for Heuristic Play

Elinor Goldschmeid saw that babies and toddlers needed to find out about the world, so she put 'the world in a basket'. (This phrase is worth remembering when putting a treasure basket together).

Objects in a treasure basket will be 'mouthed' by a baby so they need to be safe and not too small. The child should be able to use one hand or both hands to pick up individual objects. The items should not be heavy. Children should never be left alone when exploring a treasure basket.

Make up treasure basket collections ready for use and keep them in drawstring bags so there is plenty of variety for children in your pre-school. Every baby and toddler room should have a collection for staff to use.

Some of the objects in a basket should be everyday such as: bunches of keys, big spoons, plastic cups and all kinds of kitchen utensils.

Other objects should be natural and could be pine cones, large seashells, smooth pieces of wood and everyday objects made of wood such as a mug tree or kitchen-roll holder.

Textiles and pieces of materials should be in the basket: items such as a tea towel, fleece, piece of leather, woolly hat and soft blanket, etc. To enhance the experience some of the materials can be lightly scented with lavender or other light oil or perfume (remember it may be 'mouthed').

Babies and toddlers will concentrate as they explore the items. When they get excited and begin to make sounds and noises the practitioner could name objects and describe what the baby is doing and what the baby is touching. Use these opportunities to 'describe the world to the child'.

Puppets and persona dolls

What is a persona doll?

These are special large dolls that can be given a life of their own by practitioners and children together. Physically they can be used very like a puppet, usually by a practitioner. These dolls become a character that belongs in your pre-school, with their own personality, background stories and family likes and dislikes, just like another child.

The really special thing about these dolls is that children and staff create the many different facets of the dolls character together.

Children readily accept the dolls as friends, and often confidants to discuss worries or share jokes with.

Through stories and conversations with the doll character the children who need to find a voice often begin to talk, although it may start as a whispered conversation that only the doll can hear. Through the effective use of these dolls children will begin to explore language and issues and events that *will* lead to overall improvements in their communication and language skills. Listening skills and concentration will be developed and the child's imagination will be stimulated.

Puppets

Puppets can be made from almost anything, from a sock with button eyes to commercially bought characters which support books or television programmes.

The success of any puppet is the skill with which a practitioner uses it and the resulting way young children learn how to use them.

No formal teaching is necessary as the practitioner will be able to show by example or role model the use of puppets.

Why use puppets?

Puppets will build a child's language skills by providing a safe 'out of character' opportunity for the child to practise talking in a variety of ways. Self-expression is developed and the imagination is stimulated.

See the diagram on the following page for further ideas for practitioners to develop effective use of persona dolls and puppets within the pre-school.

Puppets are available from all of the main educational catalogues by post or can simply made by practitioners or willing parents.

Puppets by Post
PO Box 106 Welwyn Garden City
Herts AL6 0ZS
Tel: 01438 714009
www.PuppetsByPost.com

Puppets and Persona Dolls

When you purchase new dolls or puppets discuss how they are going to be introduced as well as their possible characteristics at a staff meeting. That way you will ensure consistency

Props can also be used with a puppet, for example during the telling of a story such as *The Three Bears* or when modelling how to turn the pages of a book or use a knife and fork, etc.

Separate those puppets and dolls that will be used only by practitioners and the others that can be accessed by children. Make the children's puppets available for self selecting. Staff should use the children's puppets/dolls as this will give the children new ideas and words to imitate

Encourage listening skills by making the puppet/doll whisper either to you or to a child. Keep movements and speech slow and deliberate

Keep puppets and dolls in brightly coloured drawstring bags or boxes to make them special and ensure the children look after them

Use the puppets to introduce new language, new songs or rhymes, numbers and colours, problem-solving and discussion of everyday dilemmas or difficulties such as playing and sharing

Take photographs of your puppets and dolls in everyday situations such as undertaking pre-school activities, visiting the shops or the park, etc. These provide useful talking points to use with the children.

Developing Pre-School Communication and Language, Paul Chapman Publishing © Chris Dukes and Maggie Smith, 2007

Story sacks

What is a story sack?

A story sack is a large cloth bag containing a children's book with supporting materials and props which are used to illustrate the story and make shared reading a memorable and enjoyable experience. The sack can contain soft toys of the book's main characters, and props and scenery that practitioners, parents and other adults can use with children to bring a book to life.

A story sack can be used and shared between children who are not yet readers but who know the story. Older and younger children can work side by side with either practitioners or parents, each enjoying the story and contents at their own level, and bilingual parents and children can enjoy the story without having to read the words.

In short a story sack does much to enhance any story. Children develop their listening skills alongside their vocabulary while using the sacks.

Story sacks can be commercially bought or made by practitioners or parents.

What kinds of books make the best story sacks?

▶ Those with good quality illustrations

▶ Those that are easy to read aloud and share (often with a repeated line/s or refrain)

▶ Those with the potential for many easy-to-buy/make props that can be replaced easily

▶ Those favourite of your pre-school (the ones the children want read over and over again)

▶ Fiction or non-fiction books

▶ Cloth or plastic books for babies or those children still 'mouthing'

The diagram below outlines how to make a story sack.

How to Make a Story Sack

Start with a large drawstring bag, paper carrier bag or see-through large zipped folder. This will depend on who is going to use the bag: practitioners only, practitioners and children or parents and children.

Decorate and name of the story sack using fabric pens, material or even an outline of the main character. Parents are really useful and often have many skills.

The bag should look inviting and be easy to store but it's what's inside that counts! Discuss contents at a staff meeting to get lots of ideas. There is no set format for a story sack.

Start with the favourite books that never go out of fashion like *The Very Hungry Caterpillar* or *Brown Bear, Brown Bear*, etc.

Put two copies of the book in the sack for sharing and a tape of the story being told (make your own if you need to – but remember to fill all of the side of the tape). Any related board game, video, photographs or related non-fiction book can be included.

Put related props in the sack such as soft toys, or related artefacts (fridge magnets are a good source). The aim is for the child to re-tell the story using the props. A prompt sheet for parents to use is also useful.

The soft toys of main characters don't have to be identical but should have the characters' main features such as colour, hat, big eyes, etc. Children quickly accept a non-identical prop.

Any available costumes, puppets, hats, etc. that complement the story. Plain paper and pencils could also be included for writing or drawing.

Developing Pre-School Communication and Language, Paul Chapman Publishing © Chris Dukes and Maggie Smith, 2007

Circle time

What is circle time?

This is the time when young children are together in the pre-school. Often this may be called key worker time or carpet time or even story time. But the key factor is that small groups of children have been brought together to share their play and learning with each other. *The beauty of a circle is that it allows children to see and hear everyone else.*

For the youngest children this may not be appropriate but as children grow older this becomes one of their main ways of learning and sharing with their peer group.

In primary schools circle time is often more formal with children sitting on chairs in a large circle. In the pre-school there may be occasions when activities dictate a circle or even sitting on chairs but generally what is needed is a comfortable floor space which is free from obstacles such as toys or furniture and any other distractions.

Why do circle time?

Circle time is when young children develop their sense of belonging to the pre-school or group, when they become an active member of the pre-school community. Some of them will find it hard and practitioners often need to offer one-on-one support and guidance. Practitioners should remember that children should not be expected to sit in one place listening for more than a few minutes and this should be reflected in planning. Those children who find sitting hard to do will often initially watch circle time from afar or be offered alternative activities until they are ready to join the group.

In circle time children are encouraged to:

▶ listen and follow instructions

▶ develop empathy and good listening

▶ build confidence when speaking

▶ learn to read non-verbal signs

▶ modify their use of tone and voice, e.g. whispering

▶ learn new words

▶ raise their self-esteem

▶ respond to story and rhyme

▶ share their personal experience

▶ consider big themes and learn the language of friendships, sharing and feelings.

In the diagram below are ideas for some circle time activities that promote the development of communication and language.

Circle Time Activities

Everybody do this
Following instructions
A practitioner holding a persona doll singing 'Everybody do this …'

What I see
Describing feelings and listening to each other
Place a piece of 'special material' on the floor. Place photographs of faces expressing emotions or illustrated pictures. Children go onto the material, choose a photograph and describe it to the others.

Old MacDonald
Listening to and following a rhythm
Using musical instruments or home-made instruments sing 'Old MacDonald had a band …'

Telephone rings
Speaking and listening and getting to know each other
Pass a telephone around the circle: the children have to pass it to the person next to them saying either the child's name or 'It's for you …'

The toy shop
Vocabulary and turn-taking
Have a selection of toys on a tray and going around the circle let each child choose one, reminding them of its name if you need to.

Pass a shopping bag around the circle with each child saying 'I went to the toy shop and I bought …'

An extended version is where they say the name of the toy the previous child has placed in the bag as well as their own.

How do you do?
Talking out loud and making friends
Start the circle by turning to the child next to you, shaking their hand and saying 'How do you do? I'm …' In turn the handshake should be passed around the circle.

The same game can be played passing a smile, a hug or even a teddy or doll saying 'This is teddy, can you give him to …'

Chinese whispers
Listening and modifying tone of voice
Start the circle by whispering a word or even a short sentence to the child next to you. The whisper is passed around the circle. The last child is encouraged to say the word/sentence out loud, and then the practitioner says the original word/sentence out loud. How do they compare?

Developing Pre-School Communication and Language, Paul Chapman Publishing © Chris Dukes and Maggie Smith, 2007

Recommended watching

Heuristic Play with Objects, video, National Children's Bureau: www.ncb.org.uk.

 ## Further reading

Hughes, A. M. (2006) *Developing Play for the Under Threes: The Treasure Basket and Heuristic Play*. David Fulton.

Mortimer, H. (1998) *Learning Through Play Circle Time*. Scholastic.

Sharp, E. (2005) *Learning Through Talk in the Early Years: Practical Activities for the Classroom*. Paul Chapman Publishing.

CHAPTER TEN
Meeting individual needs (with case studies)

In this chapter you will find:

▶ An overview of factors which can affect a child's language or communication

▶ The five steps to plan for a child's needs

▶ Case studies and strategies to outline common difficulties

▶ 'Let's Talk About …' leaflets

Overview

There are increasing numbers of children being identified with difficulties in the development of language and communication. Some of this rise may be explained by increased awareness among both practitioners and parents of the issues and importance of language in the early years. Difficulties which might have previously gone unnoticed are therefore being identified and addressed at a far earlier stage. Others might argue that the modern world, children's lifestyle, and the ways in which they spend their leisure time also contribute to the growth of language difficulties.

There is rarely one single factor which affects language and communication and each individual child will have a unique set of circumstances, influences and abilities which interact and combine to contribute to their development.

For children with identified needs with speech, language or communication it may be appropriate to write an Individual Education Plan or IEP. This is a plan which sets targets for individual children and details strategies, actions and resources which are needed to help the child achieve those targets. In this way progress can be planned for, monitored and measured.

Professionals involved with individual children, such as speech and language therapists, can give advice on target-setting and strategies. Additional support is usually available through local authority advisory services such as area special needs/inclusion coordinators (Area SENCOs).

What Should You Do If You Have Concerns About a Child's Speech, Language or Communication?

Step 1

Carry out some observations which focus directly on speech, language and communication.

Step 2

Talk to other staff and gather information about the child's speech, language and communication in different situations and circumstances (See 'Questions to Ask' sheet).

Step 3

Speak to parents and ask their opinion on their child's development.

Be specific about your concerns and use your observations to give examples of what you mean.

Step 4

Plan together how you are going to support the child. This may be through writing a play plan or an Individual Education Plan (IEP).

With parents' consent you may also seek advice from advisory staff who visit your pre-school such as area special needs coordinators (SENCOs) or curriculum advisory teachers.

Step 5

Review progress and consider with parents whether or not a referral to a speech and language therapist is appropriate. It is always better to err on the side of caution and refer any child you are concerned about.

Referrals to speech and language therapy can be made by:

GP
Health visitor
Parent
Pre-school (with parents' permission)

 Developing Pre-School Communication and Language, Paul Chapman Publishing © Chris Dukes and Maggie Smith, 2007

Observing a Child's Speech, Language and Communication: Questions to Ask Yourself

How?

How did they communicate?

For example, was speech clear? Did the child use gesture, facial expression, signs? Did they change their tone of voice or pitch?

Who?

To whom did the child speak? With whom did they interact?

For example, with practitioner or peer/individual or group.

What?

What did they actually say?

For example, did they babble, use words, phrases, sentences, questions?

What did they understand?

For example, did they follow an instruction, answer a question or comply with a request?

Where?

Where did this take place/the context?

For example, in the home corner with two other children/outside, etc.

When?

When did they speak?

For example, were they initiating interaction, answering, talking alongside other(s) or to themselves?

Why?

What was the purpose of the interaction and were they successful in their aim?

For example, were they trying to join in with another child's play or expressing a need?

If not, why not?

What was the reason the child was unsuccessful in their communication?

For example, they were not understood or did not understand, too quiet, did not have the vocabulary, etc.

 Developing Pre-School Communication and Language, Paul Chapman Publishing © Chris Dukes and Maggie Smith, 2007

Case studies to illustrate common language difficulties in the pre-school

On the following pages are case studies which illustrate some common situations found in the pre-school, with some accompanying strategies which may be helpful.

In general strategies which are helpful for those children who are experiencing difficulties with language or communication can also benefit all children. Many of the ideas proposed in the following case studies will become second nature to an experienced practitioner. More specific suggestions, such as visual timetables or planners, can still be incorporated into a practitioner's everyday work and used with a variety of children. Makaton signing, which some may think of as a more specialist skill, can be used successfully with whole pre-schools, to enrich the language and communication of even the youngest children, as shown by the huge interest in 'baby signing'.

 Case Study

Hannah is 3¹/₂ years old. She took several weeks to settle into the nursery. At first she would not join in with any activities but stood on the edge of the group watching intently what the other children did. After three months Hannah now does join in with some activities but **speaks to the other children or members of staff only in a whisper**. At home Hannah chats to her mother about the nursery and her mother has no concerns about her language.

Useful strategies

▶ Make sure that the whole group sings and has plenty of opportunities to participate in action rhymes.

▶ It is likely that Hannah will join in when the spotlight is not on her as an individual. When she does join in avoid eye contact and do not draw attention to it.

▶ Give Hannah opportunities to join in quiet, paired or small group games and activities. Listening games, lotto, hunt the animal or simple ball games will help with turn-taking and building confidence.

▶ Encourage Hannah to join in with noisy group games like 'What's the Time Mr Wolf?'.

▶ Read stories with predictable language and join-in choruses or lines, such as 'We're Going on a Bear Hunt' or stories where the children can provide the sound effects.

▶ Give opportunities for pretend play with telephones, tape recorders and microphones.

▶ Introduce puppets and masks as a way of giving Hannah a chance to use her voice through the puppet and without being seen.

Case Study

Nina has **poor understanding of language and finds any listening activity difficult**. At story or carpet times she concentrates for only one or two minutes and then begins touching or talking to the children around her.

Useful strategies

▶ Make sure that stories are kept simple and have high levels of motivation to hold Nina's interest. Lift-the-flap books or those which have puppets or toy characters are ideal.

▶ The visual cues and props which accompany stories should be available for the children to look at and use before and after the story time session. Children then have time to handle and become familiar with the characters or objects and can use them in their own play.

▶ In this way opportunities can be taken to introduce the story, characters and props to Nina before story time so that she has a degree of understanding already when she joins the whole group.

▶ Have an adult support Nina at story time. They should sit next to Nina and quietly explain and encourage her to listen. This may help to sustain her interest and understanding.

▶ Try activities to build up Nina's listening skills and concentration. Action songs and rhymes are fun and also require good listening skills. Music tapes and headphones can be used as an independent activity perhaps in the book area.

▶ Have clear but realistic expectations for carpet or story time and make sure that the sessions are an appropriate length.

▶ The Golden Rules can be useful in making explicit to children what is expected of them. These can be reinforced with visual cues such as gestures and prompt cards.

▶ Use lots of 'labelled' praise for those children who are behaving appropriately rather than drawing attention to those who are not, e.g. praise the child sitting next to Nina for 'good listening' or 'good sitting'.

▶ Acknowledge that Nina may not yet be ready or able to sit for the entire story time with the rest of the group. Have a quiet and perhaps related activity available in the room that she can go to or be guided to.

Case Study

Louise does **not seem able to follow any instructions and rarely responds** when she is spoken to. She always seems to be the last child to wash her hands, collect her snack and hang up her coat, etc. and staff are beginning to become concerned about her.

Useful strategies

▶ Suggest to Louise's parents that she has a hearing check to rule out any hearing difficulties. A health visitor or GP can organise this.

▶ Make sure that you have Louise's attention before giving any instructions. Say her name and make eye contact before speaking so that you know she is listening.

▶ If making eye contact is difficult for Louise try playing games which encourage this or simple techniques like holding objects up at your eye level when you speak which naturally draw a child's attention to your eyes.

▶ Simplify your language so that you say only the key words necessary. For example, 'Come over here and hang your coat up on the peg Louise' becomes 'Louise, come here and hang up your coat'.

▶ It is possible that you may have to give only one instruction at a time, for example: 'Louise, come here'. Then: 'Hang up your coat'.

▶ Use gestures, tone of voice and expressions to help support your language and convey additional meaning.

▶ Play very short listening games that involve a degree of anticipation so that Louise is waiting and alert to what is being said, e.g. Ring o' Roses, Ready Steady Go, etc.

▶ Ask Louise to help give out the snacks or be first to wash her hands so that you break the cycle of her always being last.

▶ Reward Louise with lots of praise when she does follow an instruction so that she wants to repeat the experience.

Case Study

Jesse is 3½ years old and a non-identical twin. She is attending speech and language therapy for **articulation difficulties**. Jesse is very lively and her speech is difficult for staff and other children to understand, particularly if she becomes excited. She loves dressing up and playing in the home corner. Her sister also attends the nursery and has no difficulties with speech.

Useful strategies

▶ Obviously make sure that you liaise with the speech and language therapist who is working with Jesse.

▶ Therapists will often provide suggestions for activities and exercises that can be done with the whole nursery group but which will particularly benefit a specific child.

▶ Practitioners often talk of being able to 'tune in' to a child with articulation difficulties and other children certainly do. Acknowledge, show interest in and accept what Jesse says even if you do not completely understand it.

▶ Give Jesse extra time to respond to you, leaving space for her to think and give her answer when she is ready.

▶ Encourage Jesse to slow down, especially when she is excited, so that her speech will be clearer.

▶ Play alongside and comment on, describe and explain activities so that Jesse hears language modelled correctly.

▶ Do not correct Jesse if she makes a mistake when speaking. Instead repeat any word which she mispronounces so that she hears how it should sound but do not ask her to repeat it.

▶ Remember that children need confidence to be able to communicate well, especially if they are having some difficulties. Try to build up confidence in all areas so that children feel they are valued and are willing to try.

Let's Talk About ...

Twins and Language and Communication

Although there are always exceptions to the rule, identical twins usually have very similar speech, language and social development as each other. Non-identical twins or fraternal twins can differ from each other in the same way as any two siblings would.

Key points

▶ There are varying degrees of closeness and dependency between twins which mean that while they are happy to communicate with each other, they can sometimes be shy or reticent when communicating with peers or adults.

▶ When talking to each other twins will often use simpler language and fewer words than when talking to adults.

▶ One twin can sometimes begin to speak for both. (This should generally be discouraged.)

▶ Some twins, especially those with immature language or speech and language difficulties, develop 'twin language'.

▶ Twins are often delayed in their speech and language development. Contributory factors can be premature birth and/or receiving less individual attention to develop verbal skills.

▶ Twins often learn about sharing and taking turns earlier than single children.

Useful strategies

▶ Take advantage of opportunities to speak to each twin individually.

▶ Give instructions separately.

▶ Create opportunities to play with or do activities with each twin at different times.

▶ Praise each child individually and be specific about what you are pleased with.

▶ When playing or doing an activity with both twins together make sure that each child has a chance to have a short conversation with you before the other child has their turn.

▶ Foster individuality by asking each child to make simple choices, about what to eat or wear for example.

▶ Give space for each twin to develop their own preferences for which stories to read, what to play, who to play with, etc.

Developing Pre-School Communication and Language, Paul Chapman Publishing © Chris Dukes and Maggie Smith, 2007

Case Study

Aaron is 3½ years old and recently staff have noticed that he seems to have **difficulties in starting a sentence** – sometimes it is several seconds before any sounds come out.

Aaron also tends to repeat parts of words such as 'Te te te te teddy' or stops half way through what he is saying. Parents have concerns too and are worried that he might be developing a stammer.

Useful strategies

▶ Observe when the stammering occurs as this can be useful information, for example when the child is excited, tired, talking to unfamiliar adults, at home or in the pre-school.

▶ Encourage the child to slow down when they speak.

▶ Slow down your own speech so that the pace of conversation is easy and not rushed.

▶ Allow plenty of time for a child to reply or answer a question.

▶ Make sure you let the child know that you are interested and listening to what they say, e.g. by nodding, making eye contact, etc.

▶ Use short simple sentences when speaking to the child.

▶ Build confidence by praising the child for playing well or completing an activity.

▶ Try to have a few minutes quiet one-on-one time with the child each day to chat in a relaxed atmosphere about what they have done or are doing.

▶ Refer to a speech and language therapist as soon as possible – early intervention can prevent difficulties later on.

Let's Talk About ...

Dysfluency or Stammering

Some facts about stammering

▶ Stammering includes repeating parts of words or whole words, not being able to start a sentence clearly and stopping half way through sentences.

▶ Different situations will affect how or if a child stammers, factors such as whether they are talking to a familiar adult or stranger, whether the environment is calm and quiet or noisy and rushed, or how the child is feeling – tired, unwell, excited or anxious.

▶ Children sometimes stammer for a period of time and then stop, only to start again after a few days, weeks or months.

▶ It is normal for a child between the ages of 2 and 5 to repeat, hesitate and stumble over their words when they are learning to talk.

▶ About 5 per cent of children of this age, mainly boys, will stammer for a while and then outgrow it naturally.

▶ A third of these children will continue to have difficulties with fluency and benefit from input from a speech and language therapist.

▶ Early intervention is very important and can prevent difficulties later on. Speak to a health visitor, GP or refer direct to the local Speech and Language Therapy Service.

(Source: The British Stammering Association, 2006)

The following excellent information leaflets are available from the British Stammering Association: ***Does your young child stammer?*** and ***How to help the child who stammers*** (referral information for professionals).

 Developing Pre-School Communication and Language, Paul Chapman Publishing © Chris Dukes and Maggie Smith, 2007

Case Study

Barry does **not speak at all in the pre-school**, either to his peers or to the staff. At home Barry will speak to his parents and brother but not to any other relatives. He dislikes any change in routine and can become anxious. The family have recently moved house and Barry has a new baby sister.

According to his mother Barry's speech and language seems to be developing well and the nursery reports that he is making age-appropriate progress in other areas of learning.

Useful strategies

▶ Play alongside Barry and give a running commentary on what you are doing. This ensures that Barry hears the language he needs but does not feel under pressure to use it himself.

▶ Encourage Barry to communicate his needs or wants non-verbally, by pointing or other gestures. Offering Barry two choices of snacks/drinks/puzzles, etc. provides a good opportunity to do this.

▶ Practise activities which use the mouth but do not require speech such as blowing bubbles, balloons, whistles or musical instruments and blowing through straws.

▶ Talk in whispers to try to encourage Barry to reply quietly. If he doesn't answer continue as if he had replied and then move on without comment.

▶ Make sure that Barry has opportunities to express himself in other ways through painting, drawing or other creative activities.

▶ Look into the possibility of the parents coming into the pre-school once a week to work with their child, and/or the child's key worker visiting the home to share a book or toy.

▶ Support parents at this difficult time – they may blame themselves for Barry's lack of speech at pre-school.

▶ With the parents' permission seek advice from a speech and language therapist or an educational psychologist. There may be an underlying emotional difficulty which needs to be addressed.

Let's Talk About ...

Selective or Elective Mutism

What is it?

Selective mutism is an emotional disorder whereby children will speak freely only in certain situations. At other times, in other situations or with certain people they remain completely silent. It can begin when children are very young, and can be triggered by events or periods of change, such as starting school or spending time in hospital. It usually is a transitory condition which only rarely lasts throughout a child's schooling.

Key points

▶ Some children make age-appropriate progress in all areas of development which do not require speech.

▶ Some children may have delayed language development.

▶ Children may avoid or have limited eye contact.

▶ Can appear withdrawn or anxious.

▶ Some communicate non-verbally with gesture or signs.

▶ It is often linked with social anxiety, anger or manipulation.

▶ Help should be sought from a speech and language therapist and/or educational psychologist.

Useful strategies

▶ Do not pressurise the child to speak.

▶ Praise any vocalisation such as noises or singing in any situation.

▶ Accept and encourage non-verbal communication such as nodding, smiling or gestures.

▶ Use every opportunity to boost the child's self-esteem.

▶ Play games which involve turn-taking but not necessarily any speech, for example, simple ball, games or action games.

▶ Try some activities which involve using the mouth, such as blowing bubbles or musical instruments.

▶ Puppets or persona dolls can be useful as the child may feel able to talk 'through' the puppet.

▶ Encourage participation in noisy games or activities as part of a group so the child is not singled out.

▶ Use a tape recorder to tape the child in order to help with assessment of language skills.

(Source: Selective Mutism Information and Research Association (SMIRA)).

Case Study

Tom is 3½ years old and has been at the nursery for a couple of months. He is **very quiet and has been heard to say only one or two single words**. He makes very limited eye contact and is often described as having a blank expression. He sits mainly on the play mat playing with trains and cars, as he does at home. He is very reluctant to try any new activities and can become distressed if an adult tries to move him away from the play mat. Staff are concerned that he is not experiencing a range of activities and the associated language and that he is not having any interaction with his peers.

Useful strategies

▶ Rather than trying to move Tom away from the play mat take an activity that you would like him to try and play with it next to him on the mat. In this way he can watch and see what you are doing without feeling threatened or as if he has to participate.

▶ When you are playing alongside him make sure that you are constantly commenting on, describing and explaining what you are doing in simple repetitive language. In this way Tom will hear the language connected to the activity even if he does not use it himself.

▶ As Tom becomes familiar with the activity offer him opportunities to join in or take turns with you, even if you do the majority of the activity and let him do the final part to complete it. This will give him the chance to experience success and you will be able to praise and encourage him.

▶ Try to incorporate cars or trains into other activities. Different kinds of vehicles can be put into the sand for example, and may encourage him to broaden his play and opportunities for language development.

▶ Gradually introduce Tom to a *visual timetable*. Two familiar activities would be enough to begin with and then, as he gains confidence, try to add a less familiar activity for him to try. His favourite choice would be the last activity so that he has a goal to work towards.

▶ Try using simple gestures or signs to accompany speech. Makaton signs for early words are very close to natural gestures and are easy to learn. They can be useful for all children to help them communicate and support their speech.

▶ Talk to Tom's parents about a referral to a speech and language therapist. More expert advice on signing can be given if appropriate.

▶ A developmental check with a paediatrician may also be necessary.

Let's Talk About ...

Visual Timetables

A visual timetable is a pictorial way of showing children what is happening in their day. Young children have little sense of time, so a set of photographs, pictures or real objects to represent different activities or times of the day can be very helpful in showing the routine of the pre-school and the sequence of activities.

It can be used in many different ways:

▶ with the whole pre-school group as a reminder of what is happening throughout the day – this promotes independence and is particularly useful for 'changeover' times;

▶ with small groups who perhaps need the security and confidence of knowing what is happening next or who find it hard to choose activities;

▶ with individuals who have specific targets or who need guiding between activities or help with concentration or behaviour.

Planning and preparation are essential. Make sure that you have a clear purpose for using the timetable and that all staff understand how you intend it to be used. Once you have a set of photographs or objects they can be pinned on the wall, hung on a washing line or fixed to card with Velcro strips.

Useful tips

▶ Keep it simple.

▶ Make sure it is displayed at a child's eye level.

Let's Talk About ...

Augmentative and Alternative Communication

For some children who have difficulties with learning to speak, understanding and making themselves understood, the world can be a frustrating place not only for them but also for the adults who care for them. For these children speech and language therapists may suggest the use of other methods of communication to supplement or replace speech. These methods are known as augmentative and alternative communication (AACs) and include signs, symbols and pictures.

The most common signing systems are:

▶ **British Sign Language** (BSL). This is the language used by the deaf or hearing impaired.

▶ **Makaton and Signalong** These are systems used by children with a whole range of needs or difficulties. 'Signing' involves making particular gestures which represent words.

Makaton and Signalong both use the sign alongside the spoken word to

- help children both understand what is being said and to
- encourage their own language development.
- Makaton also has a set of accompanying symbols.

Another example of a symbol system is:

▶ **Picture Exchange Communication System** (PECS)
This is based on the child exchanging a picture card for something which they want or need. Some children can eventually build up whole sentences with which to communicate.

Other forms of augmentative and alternative communication are:

▶ **Voice Output Communication Aids** (VOCAs)
These are various devices which speak. This can be anything from those that produce single words and sentences to those that turn text into speech. They are usually activated by some sort of switch. Simple versions can be introduced to children at a very early stage using switch-activated toys for example.

Advice on AACs and VOCAs will be available from speech and language therapists and other professionals working with individual children.

Further reading and support

▶ www.ace-centre.org.uk

▶ www.Britishsignlanguage.com

▶ www.signalong.org.uk

▶ www.makaton.org

 Developing Pre-School Communication and Language, Paul Chapman Publishing © Chris Dukes and Maggie Smith, 2007

Further reading

Hull Learning Service (2004) *Supporting Children with Speech and Language Difficulties*. David Fulton.

Mortimer, H. (2007) *Special Needs in the Early Years: Speech and Language Difficulties*. Scholastic.

APPENDIX A

Useful contacts

Association for All Speech Impaired Children (AFASIC)
2nd floor, 50–52 Great Sutton Street
London EC1V 0DJ
020 7490 9410
www.afasic.org.uk

British Stammering Association
15 Old Ford Road
London E2 9PJ
0208 983 1003
www.stammering.org

BT Education Programme – 'The Better World' campaign
Free resources including *Make Chatter Matter* DVD and posters
www.bt.com/education

Department for Children, Schools and Families (DCSF)
www.direct.gov.uk

ICAN (national charity for children with speech and language impairments)
4 Dyers Building
London EC1N 2OP
0870 010 40 66
www.ican.org.uk

Makaton Development Project
31 Firwood Drive
Camberley, Surrey
GU15 3QD
Tel 01276 61390
www.makaton.org

National Autistic Society (NAS)

393 City Road

London EC1V 1NE

0207 833 2299

www.nas.org.uk

National Deaf Children's Society (NDCS)

15 Dufferin Street

London EC1Y 8UR

0207 460 8658

www.ndcs.org.uk

National Literacy Trust

www.literacytrust.org.uk

Royal College of Speech and Language Therapists

2 White Hart Yard

London SE1 1NX

0207 378 1200

www.rcslt.org.uk

Royal National Institute for the Blind (RNIB)

105 Judd Street

London WC1H 9NE

0845 766 9999

www.rnib.org.uk

Selective Mutism Information and Research (SMIRA)

13 Humberstone Drive

Leicester LE5 0RE

0116 212 7411

Talk to Your Baby

www.talktoyourbaby.org.uk

Crossword solution

```
        ¹B          ²B
   ³J  A  R  G  O  N
        B           D
 ⁵P     B           Y      ⁴B        ⁶V           ⁷S
  R     L                   B         O    ⁸S      I
  O     I                   B         C     Y  ⁹A  G
¹⁰N  O  N  V  E  R  B  A  L  A         A     L  U  N
  U     G                   L         B     L  D  I
  N              ¹¹A  R  T  I  C  U  L  A  T  I  O  N
  C                         N         L     B  T  G
  I                         G         A     A  O
¹²L  A  N  G  U  A  G  E               R     A  R
  T                                   Y     L  Y
  I
¹³M  O  T  H  E  R  E  S  E
  N
```

Across

3 jargon

10 non-verbal

12 *see 2 down*

11 articulation

13 motherese

Down

1 babbling

2 *and* **12** *across* body language

4 modelling

5 pronunciation

6 vocabulary

7 signing

8 syllable

9 auditory

Developing Pre-School Communication and Language, Paul Chapman Publishing © Chris Dukes and Maggie Smith, 2007

References

Boyer, E. L. (1991) *Ready to Learn: A Mandate for the Nation*. Princeton, NJ: Carnegie Foundation.

Britton, J. (1972) *Language and Learning*. London: Pelican.

Crystal, D. (1987) *Cambridge Encyclopaedia of Knowledge*. Cambridge: Cambridge University Press.

Petrie, P. (1997) *Communicating with Children and Adults*. London: Arnold.

Rouse Selleck, D. (1995) *Managing to Change. Module 4: Playing and Learning*. London: National Children's Bureau.

St Augustine [354–430] (1963) *The Confessions of St Augustine* (ed. Rex Warner). New York: Penguin.

Whitehead, M. (2002) *Developing Language and Literacy with Young Children*. London: Hodder & Stoughton.

SWINDON COLLEGE

LEARNING RESOURCE CENTRE

Index